Feathered Star Quilts

by Marsha McCloskey

Feathered Star Productions, Seattle, Washington

Title page: **Amish Feathered Star** by Margaret Mathisson, 1986,
Bainbridge Island, Washington, 81" x 96". (Collection of the artist)

FEATHERED STAR QUILTS
© Marsha Reynolds McCloskey 1987
All rights reserved.

Feathered Star Productions
2151 7th Avenue West
Seattle, Washington 98119
Phone/Fax 206-283-5214

Printed in the USA
99 98 97 96 95   7 6 5 4 3

ISBN: 0-9635422-3-0

(Previously published by That Patchwork Place, Inc., Bothell,
 Washington)

CONTENTS

ACKNOWLEDGMENTS

My heartfelt thanks are extended to:

Joyce Bacon, Grace Bawtinheimer, Karoline Patterson Bresenhan, Patricia Boyer, Beverly Bynum, Franklin and Mary Daenzer, Donna Hanson Eines, John Flynn, Helen Frost, Imogene Gooch, Jan Halgrimson, Bryce Hamilton, Suzanne Hammond, Lindsay Horton, Gay Imbach, Roger and Keiko Keyes, Louise Kindig, Judy Martin, Judy and Jack Mathieson, Lois Odell, Bets Ramsey, Linda Reuther, James and Barbara Rickey, Phyllis Saelens, Nancy Sheafe, Marie Shirer, Al and Merry Silber, Julie Silber, Judy Sogn, Valerie Valaas, and Sharon Yenter, who graciously loaned their quilts to be photographed or gave permission for transparencies of their quilts to be used in this book.

Mary Barton, Jinny Beyer, Barbara Brackman, Richard Cleveland, Kathy Cook, Sharyn Craig, Ruby L. Davis, Helen Ericson, Joyce Gross, Glendora Hutson, Judy Mathieson, Rosalie Pfieffer, Marguerite Weibusch, and all the other quilters and researchers who spent time talking, showed me quilts, shared slides, opened their quilt libraries, and wrote innumerable letters to help with my research.

The following deserve special thanks for their help and cooperation:

DAR Museum, Washington, D.C.
Steve Tuttle, Photographer, and Gloria Seaman Allen, Curator, transparencies of two quilts from the DAR collection: #7020 Feathered Star and #62.27 Feathered Star by Marietta Pierce.

Shelburne Museum, Shelburne, Vermont
Transparencies of two quilts from their collection: #10-169, Star Spangled Banner and #10-349, Feathered Star.

Museum of History and Industry, Seattle, Washington
Howard Giske, Photographer, and Lois Bark, Curatorial Assistant, transparency of the Tingle Feathered Star.

Oregon Historical Society, Portland, Oregon
Transparencies of OHS 62-377 Feathered Star Variation, OHS 72-94.11 Feathered Star Variation, and OHS 63-58 Twinkling Star.

Yakima Valley Museum and Historical Society, Yakima, Washington
Ann Troianello, Project Chairman, *A Common Thread, Quilts in the Yakima Valley,* slide of first Flower Wreath and Stars quilt.

Warren County Historical Society, Lebanon, Ohio
Permission to use E. P. Dutton transparency of Hunt Family Feathered Star.

American Hurrah Antiques, New York, New York
Kate Kopp, transparency of second Flower Wreaths and Stars quilt.

Stearns Technical Textiles Company, Cincinnati, Ohio
Pam Campbell and Pam Reising, transparency of Imogene Gooch's Feathered Star quilt.

Austin Area Quilt Guild, Austin, Texas
Slide of 1984 Donation quilt.

East Bay Heritage Quilters, Albany, California
Transparencies of six Feathered Star quilts from their 1982 show catalog, *Quilts, a Tradition of Variations.*

University of Texas Press, Austin, Texas
Five transparencies from *Lone Stars: A Legacy of Texas Quilts 1836-1936* by Karoline Patterson Bresenhan and Nancy O'Bryant Puentes.

The Quilt Digest Press, San Francisco, California
Michael Kile, editor, transparency of red and white Triple Feathered Star from *The Quilt Digest-3.*

Quilter's Newsletter Magazine. Wheatridge, Colorado
Transparencies of Imogene Gooch's Feathered Star Sampler, Marsha McCloskey's Christmas Radiant Star Banner, and Judy Martin's Fine Feathered Star from the cover of *Quiltmaker* magazine.

E. P. Dutton, Inc., New York, New York
Cyril Nelson, editor, transparencies from 1980, 1981, and 1983 *Quilt Engagement Calendars* and one from the *Quilt Engagement Calendar Treasury.*

INTRODUCTION

The first section of this book explores the many Feathered Star block variations and explains how and why they differ. It also covers traditional sets and border treatments.

The second section concentrates on Feathered Star quilts, old and new, and how the pattern may have evolved. Gathered here are examples of some of the finest Feathered Star quilts in existence. I hope you share my excitement in seeing so many photographs of Feathered Star quilts in one place, in reading their histories, and in finding out how they fit into the larger framework of traditional American quiltmaking.

How to piece a Feathered Star block is explained in the third section of this book. Piecing Feathered Star blocks, although sometimes time-consuming, is not particularly difficult and can go faster with quick piecing methods such as bias-strip piecing, described on page 56. The lavender Feathered Star with Pineapple Border shown here was, in fact, pieced on the sewing machine in just ten hours. The pattern and instructions for this quilt are found on page 101.

You will find twenty patterns for Feathered Star blocks in the pattern section. These blocks have been drafted and tested especially for this book. They fit together properly and

you needn't worry about fudging for accuracy.

For those of you who are just itching to get started on a Feathered Star quilt but who don't want to design your own just now, the next section includes complete instructions for several Feathered Star quilts and projects. For those quilters who have tried in the past to draft their own Feathered Star patterns, only to run into seemingly unsolvable problems of geometry, and who are still curious, I have included a section on Drafting the Feathered Star which begins on page 114.

The book concludes with a Glossary of Techniques, a brief but thorough overview of the steps in making a quilt. Also, take a moment to read the Bibliography and Acknowledgments. The books and articles listed are excellent sources of quilt history, patterns, and techniques. The people mentioned in the Acknowledgments are as important to the existence of this book as any other part. The help and support I have received from the nationwide quilting community has been both amazing and gratifying.

I hope you use this book and enjoy it. It is the resource I was looking for and could not find five years ago, when I first became fascinated by Feathered Stars.

Feathered Star with Pineapple Border by Marsha McCloskey, 1986, Seattle, Washington, 65" x 65". This simple medallion quilt takes only ten hours to piece on the sewing machine. Inspired by the antique child's quilt pictured on page 25, this pattern works especially well in large floral prints. Instructions begin on page 101. (Mildred L. Reynolds, Redmond, Washington)

FEATHERED STARS

Variable Star or Star Spangled Banner, Charlotte, Michigan, 1899, 87" x 84". The stunning design of this quilt top is effectively emphasized by the crisscrossed border. (George E. Schoellkopf Gallery. Photo courtesy of E.P. Dutton, Inc.)

Little has been written specifically about the Feathered Star pattern or Feathered Star quilts, but there are many photographs of them in quilt books and publications. Those pictured are highly individual in style and workmanship. Color in the quilts ranges from formal two-color designs to gaily multicolored scrap quilts. If you are lucky enough to own a Feathered Star quilt from the last century, it is most likely a two-color design (blue and white, or red and white) with a great deal of fine quilting and a sawtooth border. The quilt is probably in good condition, having been kept for years as a "best quilt" or lovingly cared for as a family heirloom.

The Feathered Star is a very old quilt pattern. It has long been a favorite of American quilters. In 1929, the *Kansas City Star* offered templates for "A very old Saw-tooth Quilt" and noted that the "Sawtooth pattern is an antique among quilt blocks . . . Grandmother will remember the sawtooth pattern for it is one of the very oldest designs known." The design pictured here is a star edged with small triangles — a Feathered Star.

Of the many pieced stars in American patchwork, the Feathered Star is one of the most intricate and most loved. To achieve its twinkling beauty, each block can contain hundreds of pieces, depending on its size and complexity. Though not particularly difficult to make (only straight seams are involved), Feathered Stars have long been a benchmark of achievement for quiltmakers.

The inscription on one vintage quilt speaks eloquently of the maker's pride in her accomplishment. A Feathered Star variation quilt with four large blocks, a pieced border, and appliqued flags and stars was inscribed "D.D., Charlotte, Mich., Feb. 1899, 2,984 pieces." The quiltmaker did not put her full name on the quilt, but the number of pieces seemed important.

Further evidence that Feathered Star quilts were considered special is the amount of fine quilting — feather wreaths, plumes, stipple quilting, and trapunto — often lavished in the large, unpieced areas between blocks.

Slashed Feathered Star with Trapunto Wreaths, origin unknown, c. 1870, 80'' x 80''. The Slashed Feathered Star blocks appear to be a simplification of the Star Spangled Banner block design. (Franklin and Mary Daenzer. Photo courtesy of the East Bay Heritage Quilters)

Star Spangled Banner, origin unknown, c. 1890, 89'' x 91''. Four large blocks, lattices, and interior sawtooth borders easily fill this quilt. It is the basis for the logo of the Houston Quilt Festival. (Collection of the Houston Quilt Festival)

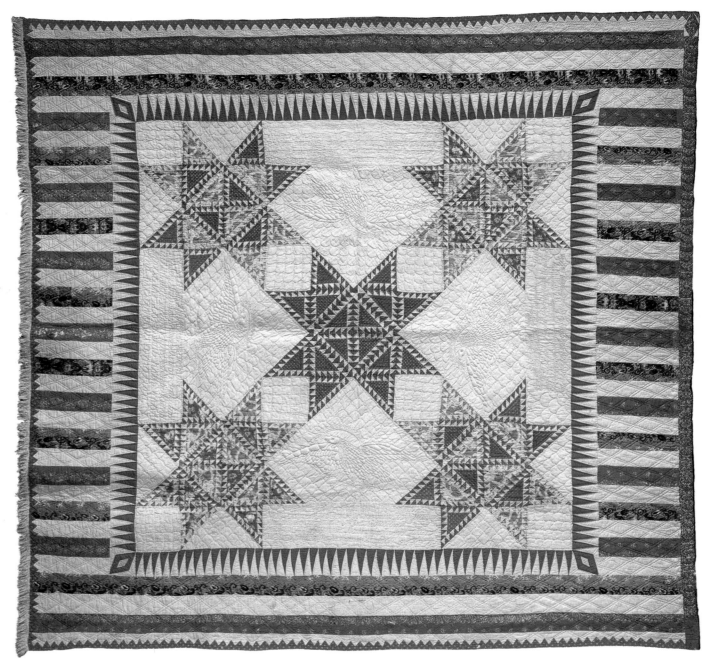

Star Spangled Banner by Mrs. Alexander Cramndin, 1840, New England, 86'' x 95''. The Star Spangled Banner block name came from this quilt. At the Henry Ford Museum in Dearborn, Michigan, where it was exhibited, in 1955, Florence Peto described it in her checklist as follows:
STAR SPANGLED BANNER. Four quilted and stuffed eagles under each four lines in quilting stitchery of the national anthem. Followed by ''F.C.(sic) Key''. Notice how the quilt has been made to look like a flag — brown staff along one edge and fringe at the opposite end.

Along the bottom edge of the quilt, stitched out in the quilting is the inscription ''Alexander Cramndin Jr. Made by his mother. 1840.'' It was probably a freedom quilt made for his 21st birthday. (Photo courtesy of the Shelburne Museum, Shelburne, Vermont)

FEATHERED STAR BLOCKS

More a category of pieced stars than one specific design, Feathered Star blocks have many variations. The names, such as Feather Edge Star, Star of Chamblie, Pine Cone, and California Star appear over and over. Often the same names are applied to different Feathered Star blocks. One Feathered Star enthusiast has catalogued over 100 different star variations.

The simplest of the Feathered Star designs contains about 120 pieces in a single block. The Radiant Star and the Star of Chamblie are simple stars; the Star Spangled Banner is the most intricate with over 600 pieces.

All Feathered Stars are based on one of three basic pieced stars: the nine-patch Variable Star, the sixteen-patch Sawtooth Star, or the Le Moyne Star with its equidistant points. The star shapes are edged with sawtooth borders of small triangles called "feathers." Sometimes the triangles form "dogtooth" instead of "sawtooth" borders. The number of triangles making up the feathers varies from one version of the design to the next. The tips of the stars can be diamonds, parallelograms, triangles, or simply blunt.

The centers, however, provide the best space for individuality of design. They can vary from a single, large unpieced square to a many-faceted Noonday Sun or Mariner's Compass. Many of today's quilters, noting the variety of possible designs, have made Feathered Star Sampler quilts in which the basic star stays the same, but the centers are changed.

Radiant Star by Marsha McCloskey, 1983, Seattle, Washington, 20" x 20". This delicate Feathered Star variation is probably the simplest of all the Feathered Star designs to piece. It is based on the Le Moyne Star, the points are true diamonds, and all the feathered triangles are the same size. (Collection of the author)

Star of Chamblie by Marsha McCloskey, 1986, Seattle, Washington, 67" x 67". Though traditional Feathered Star quilts are often worked in formal two- or three-color combinations, some of the most exciting are made of scraps. This multi-fabric treatment gives the already dynamic design a new depth and motion. (Collection of the author)

FEATHERED STAR BLOCKS

Star of Chamblie

Feather Edged Star

Radiant Star

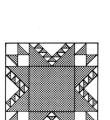

Twinkling Star

Star Spangled Banner

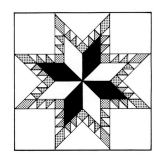

Feathered Le Moyne Star

Sawtooth Star

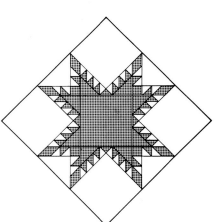

Feather Star

California Star

Feathered Star I

Feathered Variable Star

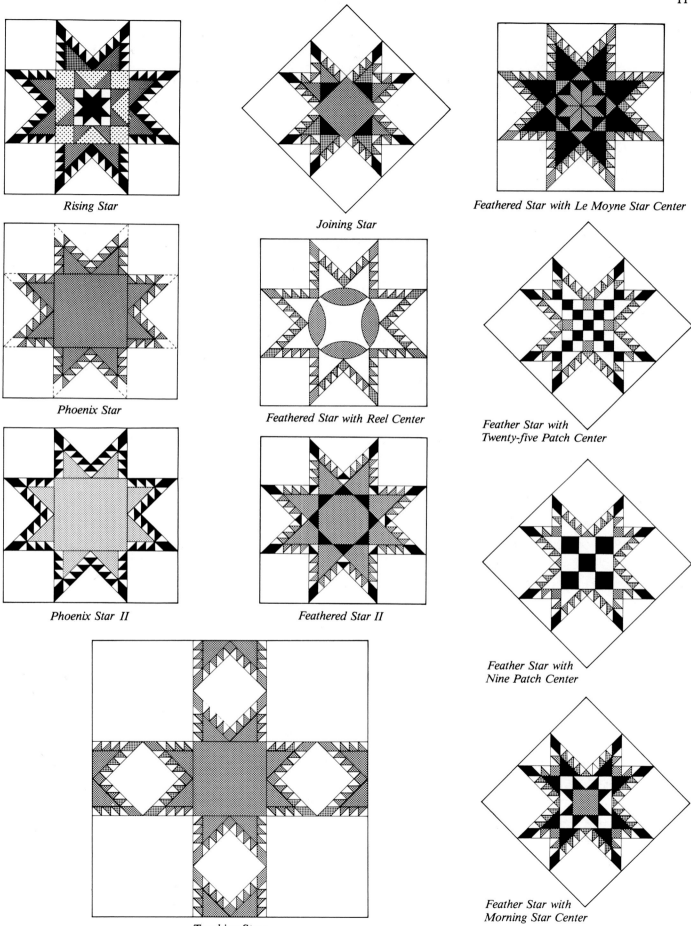

Rising Star

Joining Star

Feathered Star with Le Moyne Star Center

Phoenix Star

Feathered Star with Reel Center

Feather Star with
Twenty-five Patch Center

Phoenix Star II

Feathered Star II

Feather Star with
Nine Patch Center

Touching Stars

Feather Star with
Morning Star Center

Feathered Star Sampler by Imogene Gooch, 1983, Rockville, Indiana, 88" x 88". This quilt was made for the 1982-83 "Stars of the Star" contest sponsored by *The Indianapolis Star* and the William H. Block Company. The 12" stars inside the larger 24" Feathered Stars include Rolling Star, Maltese Star, Falling Star, Lemon Star, Mexican Star, Blazing Star, French Star, Le Moyne Star, and Morning Star. Winning seventh place in the contest it was made for, this quilt went on to win second place in the 1985 American Quilter's Society show. (Collection of the American Quilter's Society. Photo courtesy of *Quilter's Newsletter Magazine)*

Feathered Star Sampler by Marsha McCloskey, 1985, Seattle, Washington, 76" x 76". Many old Feathered Star quilts were made in only two colors. This red and white sampler was intended to look traditional but also to explore the possible variations of one Feathered Star design. (Collection of the author)

Feathered Star Sampler by Marsha McCloskey, 1986, Seattle, Washington, 45'' x 45''. (Collection of the author)

Feathered Star Sampler by Suzanne Hammond, 1986, Bellingham, Washington, 81'' x 99''. After taking a Feathered Star class from the author, the maker of this quilt spent the next three months designing and piecing this quilt top. The center of each star is a different design. The pillow blocks are variations of feathered four-pointed stars called The Philippines, Feathered World Without End, and Philadelphia Patch. (Collection of the artist)

Feathered Star with Blazing Sun Center by Mrs. Rirhood, 1896, Grandview, Iowa, 70'' x 80''. This finely quilted piece is dated but not signed. It is in good condition, although what was once dark green, has faded to a paler shade. The red, however, has retained its vibrancy. The design here is constructed not block by block, but as a bar quilt, which provides large unpieced areas for fine quilting. Notice also the use of half-blocks to bring the quilt out to proper size. (In the Beginning, Seattle, Washington)

Feathered Star with Mariner's Compass Center, maker unknown, c. 1855, Pennsylvania, 74'' x 86''. The color on the feathers of these stars is reversed — the dark triangles are on the outside. (Franklin and Mary Daenzer, photo courtesy of the East Bay Heritage Quilters)

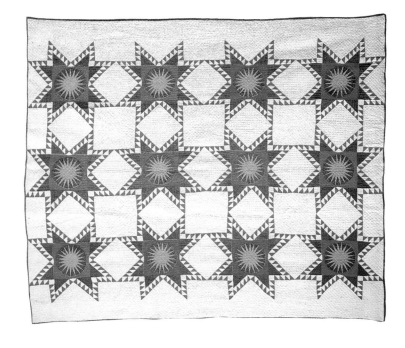

Feathered Star with Sunflower Center, maker unknown, c. 1860, Ohio, 78" x 78". Constructing her Feathered Star as a bar quilt, this quilter skillfully combined the sunflower motif in the center of her stars with harvest colors in a quilt that speaks of weather, place and season. (Mary Strickler's Quilt Collection, photo courtesy of Linda Reuther and Julie Silber)

Feathered Star with Le Moyne Star Center, origin unknown, c. 1890-1910, 72'' x 80''. This pretty Feathered Star quilt is unusual on two counts. First it has half-squares to bring it out to size; and second, the tips of the stars are split into two triangles, adding to the sparkle of the design. All the feather triangles used here are the same size, and in order to make them fit, the maker had to chop off some of the corners. (Collection of the author)

GEOMETRY OF THE BLOCKS

Feathered Stars have a reputation for being difficult. The problem is not with the piecing, which is mostly straight-seam sewing, but with the geometry involved in drafting the templates. The challenge is in getting the little feather triangles to fit evenly along all the edges of the star shape. If the base star is a Le Moyne Star, as for the Radiant Star, the legs of the star are diamonds and the same feather triangles are used throughout the block. This is because the sides of a diamond are all equal, so each side will be divisible by the same numbers. A Feathered Star based on the Le Moyne Star will have equidistant points tipped with diamonds, and the number of feathers on each side of the star legs will be equal. These diamond-based block designs have been called the true Feathered Stars.

A pieced star with points that are not equidistant is based on a grid star, a Sawtooth or Variable Star. These stars, when edged with feather triangles, have been called, not Feathered Stars, but Sawtooth Stars. It is with grid-based stars that the pattern maker runs into trouble. The legs of these stars are triangles, each with two short sides that are equal and one longer side. Little feather triangles that fit evenly along the short side of the large triangle will, most times, not fit evenly along the long side. Generally, two different-sized triangles must be drafted to allow the pattern to fit together smoothly. The difference in the two templates is often as small as 1/16'', but 1/16'' multiplied can make a big difference in fit.

While recognizing the geometric differences in the stars, I have grouped all the Sawtooth and Feathered Stars in this book under the category of Feathered Stars. If it is a star with eight points that are edged with little triangles, it is a Feathered Star. What you call a design, after all, will not change its components.

For those quilters interested in learning to draft Feathered Star designs, a section called Drafting the Feathered Star begins on page 114.

Le Moyne Star

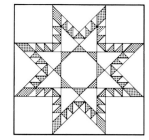

Radiant Star

Sawtooth Star

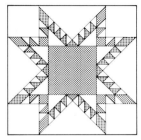

Star of Chamblie

Variable Star

Feather Edged Star

A pattern for a Feathered Christmas Star in a 1979 issue of *Lady's Circle Patchwork* began with:

> "Only the expert should tackle any Feathered Star —
> this one especially. You will find the usual inaccuracy in
> the straight and slanted rows of "feathers" or small #6
> triangles. It takes a little cheating in the stitching to make
> them work."[1]

It takes real confidence to proceed after an introduction like that! Few quilters would be anxious to try a pattern that indicated in the first two sentences that it would not fit together properly.

The makers of many old Feathered Star quilts probably did not use patterns from books and magazines but made their own templates based on pictures or quilts that they had seen. Because each quiltmaker dealt with the problems of geometry in her own way, many differences appear in the details of the stars. In many old quilts, accommodations were obviously made in the piecing for templates that did not fit.

1. *Lady's Circle Patchwork Quilts, no. 17 (1979), p.64.*

18

Feather triangles were often stretched or crowded, had points chopped off in the sewing, or involved odd-shaped pattern pieces to complete the design. Perhaps it is because so many versions of the stars required skillful fudging to make the pieces fit that the Feathered Star has not been approached with much confidence by quilters in the current quilt revival of the 1970s and 1980s.

Happily, there are Feathered Star blocks that are logical and fit together smoothly. In no way should this pattern be reserved for only the most skilled needlewomen. Many good Feathered Star patterns have been used by quilters over the years. In those included in the pattern section of this book, each template is accurate, and you will not have to "fudge" or "cheat" to make the pieces fit. Most of the designs are so straightforward and logical in their construction that they involve only straight seams and can be pieced easily on the sewing machine.

Feathered Star with Le Moyne Star Center, origin unknown,, c. 1870, 86" x 95". The maker of this quilt top obviously had problems making her stars fit together and simply added extra pieces here and there to help them along. (Helen Young Frost, Sunland, California)

OTHER FEATHERED DESIGNS

Sawtooth borders appeared early in American patchwork. Although Feathered Stars with their sawtooth edges rarely date before 1835, other feathered designs, such as Delectable Mountains, were in the American design vocabulary prior to that time.

Standard eight-pointed stars, therefore, are not the only shapes that quiltmakers have edged with sawtooth borders to make pieced designs. Amish quilters occasionally added feathers or sawtooth borders to their large-scale bars and diamonds. Delectable Mountains is made up of large triangles with sawtooth edges. Lady of the Lake is a feathered design, and Blindman's Fancy is another. There are several examples of feathered four-pointed stars, such as Pine Cone and Feathered World Without End, as well as feathered five- and six-pointed stars. John Flynn, of Billings, Montana, even drafted feather edges for the elongated star that is the center of his medallion quilt.

Delectable Mountains by Lois Odell, 1984, Kirkland, Washington, 54" x 54". This green and white wall quilt embodies the feelings of peace and plenty expressed in John Bunyan's description of the evergreen-covered new land in *Pilgrim's Progress*. The book was written in the 1600s, and the name Delectable Mountains was adopted early as a quilt pattern name in this country. (Collection of the artist)

Pine Cone, origin unknown, 70" x 84". A feathered four-pointed star, this design is also known as a Feathered World Without End and as a Pineapple. (That Patchwork Place, Inc., Bothell, Washington)

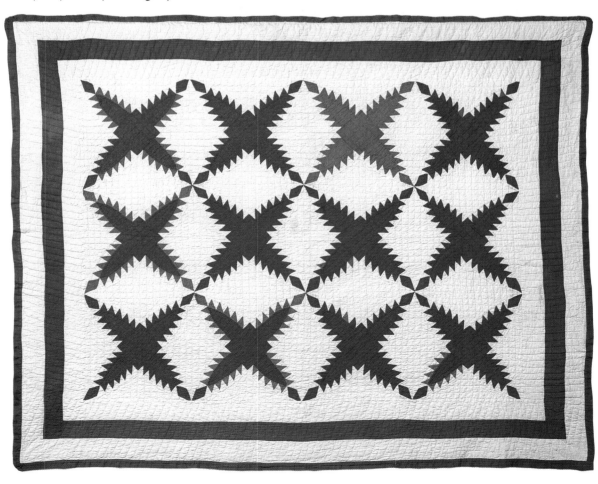

Elongated Feathered Star Medallion, by John Flynn, 1986, Billings, Montana, 91'' x 106''. (Collection of the artist)

Founders Star, made by Jewel Patterson, assisted by Helen O'Bryant, Nancy O'Bryant, and Karey Patterson Bresenhan, 1986, Houston, Texas, 104'' x 104''. Made by founders of the American International Quilt Association, this unique feathered five-pointed star medallion quilt was designed for the organization's donation quilt in celebration of the Texas Sesquicentennial. (Owned by Kathleen McCrady, photo courtesy American International Quilt Association)

SETS

Feathered Star blocks can be set next to each other or can be separated by alternate unpieced blocks or plain or pieced lattices. In this respect, they are like any other pieced design. Because of their complexity, however, Feathered Star blocks are often large, and relatively few are needed to complete a quilt top. The sawtooth edges in the blocks are visually active, and simple sets are well suited to most Feathered Stars.

The Feathered Star is also appropriate for the centers of medallion-style quilts. Indeed, many Feathered Star quilts being made today are wall hangings with single Feathered Stars in the center surrounded by complex pieced borders.

Because Feathered Star blocks are so large, quilters often have had to incorporate half-blocks at one end of a quilt to make it come out to the proper finished dimension. Old-time quilters were eminently practical, and if they wanted a quilt to be a certain size, they would simply piece until it was big enough. These Feathered Star quilts with half-blocks along the bottom or top look rather strange, out of balance, or incomplete, when viewed out flat or on a wall. But if you think of the quilts as they were designed, as bedcovers, it is a very reasonable design solution. By placing the half-blocks at the top of the bed, where they will cover the pillows or be covered by them, all the whole stars will lie on the bed.

Feather Edged Star by Lillie Ann McBee Daugherty, c. 1900, Gainesville, Texas, 67″ x 79″. The fabrics for this scrappy Feathered Star quilt were probably gathered over a period of twenty-five years from 1875-1900. The half-stars on this quilt are unusual because they fall on two sides. Perhaps the quilt was planned for a bed which would be in a corner against two walls. (From *Lone Stars: A Legacy of Texas Quilts, 1836-1936*, by Karoline Patterson Bresenhan and Nancy O'Bryant Puentes, Copyright © 1986. Courtesy of the University of Texas Press. Owned by Jessie Glynn Daugherty Burnett)

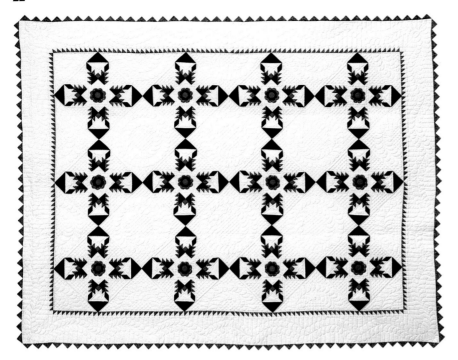

Christmas Feathered Star by Imogene Gooch, 1986, Rockville, Indiana, 74'' x 94''. This block pattern was copied from an old, worn quilt. Quilting designs, sawtooth border, and prairie points are the maker's own additions. This block pattern is a variation of the 16'' Joining Star block given on page 105. (Collection of the artist)

Sawtooth Star by Ruthie Fugate Parkey, c. 1859, Claiborne County, Tennessee, 61'' x 81½''. Green squares in the corners of these Feathered Star blocks allow the blocks to "chain," creating an overall quilt design. Plain white alternate blocks in the set provide space for extraordinary quilting. This is a bride's quilt, embellished with hearts, flowers, tulips, stars, cross-hatching, and double quilting. (From *Lone Stars: A Legacy of Texas Quilts, 1836-1936* by Karoline Patterson Bresenhan and Nancy O'Bryant Puentes, Copyright © 1986. Courtesy of the University of Texas Press. Owned by Ebb Kelly Jones and Judy Jones Puder)

Sawtooth Star by Susanah Mote Rush, c. 1880, Ennis, Texas, 76'' x 76''. Set with lattices in the same fabric as the background of the blocks, the Feathered Stars in this quilt "float." The thirteen red squares employed in the set and borders are a strong and unusual design element. (From *Lone Stars: A Legacy of Texas Quilts, 1836-1936* by Karoline Patterson Bresenhan and Nancy O'Bryant Puentes, Copyright © 1986. Photo courtesy of the University of Texas Press. Owned by Mr. and Mrs. Reagan Looney)

Feathered Star by Cynthia Jane Campbell Keith, c. 1855-1865, Dublin, Texas, 67'' x 84''. Set with strong indigo lattices and red and white nine-patch blocks, this quilt contains over 1600 hand-pieced triangles. It is quilted in straight lines about ½'' apart. (From *Lone Stars: A Legacy of Texas Quilts, 1836-1936* by Karoline Patterson Bresenhan and Nancy O'Bryant Puentes, Copyright © 1986. Courtesy of the University of Texas Press. Owned by Phillip A. Holcomb)

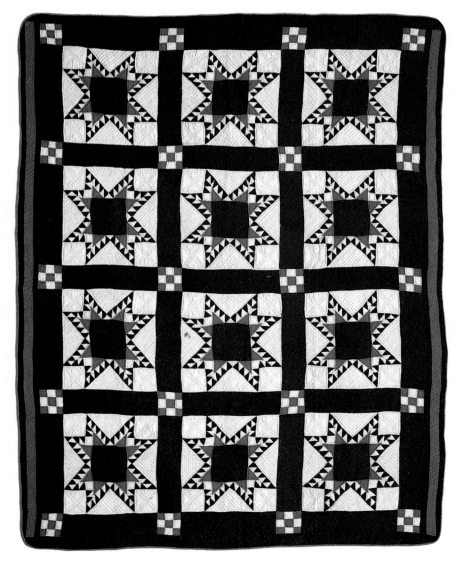

Field of Feathered Stars, maker unknown, c. 1850, Michigan, 75'' x 75''. The mini-scale of these stars is extraordinary. Each triangle is ¼'' wide, and it is beautifully quilted in ¼'' hanging diamonds. The back is homespun and the binding is handmade braiding of the type used on hems of dresses. The fabrics are home-dyed. (Al and Merry Silber. Photo courtesy of the East Bay Heritage Quilters)

Feathered Star and Irish Chain, origin unknown, c. 1850, 65'' x 82''. The Irish Chain set and scalloped edge of this quilt are very unusual. Uncommon, too, is the Reel used as the center of the Feathered Star. (Gay Imbach and Joyce Bacon)

Feathered Star Medallion with Field of Evening Stars, maker unknown, c. 1850, Ohio, 90'' x 102''. A large, yellow Feathered Star, whimsically embellished with applique leaves and flowers, is surrounded by print patches and multicolored small stars. (Mary Strickler's Quilt Collection. Linda Reuther and Julie Silber. Photo courtesy of the East Bay Heritage Quilters)

Feathered Star with Pineapple Border, origin unknown, c. 1850-1860, 33½'' x 33½''. Design, color, and quilting combine to make a completely satisfying miniature. This quilt was the inspiration for the lavender and white Feathered Star Medallion pictured on page 5. (Thomas K. Woodward: American Antiques and Quilts. Photo courtesy of E. P. Dutton, Inc.)

California Star by Donna Hanson Eines, 1984, Edmonds, Washington, 28'' x 28''. Finely quilted feather wreaths with red and green fabrics combine to make this an effective Christmas wall hanging. (Collection of the artist)

Fine Feathered Star, made by Louise Morrison, designed by Judy Martin for *Quiltmaker*, 1986, Colorado, 60¼'' x 60¼''. See page 128 for pattern ordering information for this lovely Feathered Star Medallion quilt. (Photo courtesy of *Quiltmaker* magazine)

California Medallion by Judy and Jack Mathieson, 1979, Woodland Hills, California, 102" x 102". This quilt was made by Judy with help from her husband Jack for his parents' fiftieth wedding anniversary. The California Star in the center is surrounded by a gold Double Wedding Ring border and a Road to California border. Quilting motifs include Eastern Star, Shrine, and medical and leaky faucet symbols. (Mr. and Mrs. C. J. Mathieson)

Feathered Star wall quilt by Judy Sogn, 1985, Seattle, Washington, 33" x 33". The octagonal shape of this Le Moyne Star-based Feathered Star design is emphasized and repeated by the pieced border and final shape of this small quilt. (Mr. and Mrs. Clyde Zeigler)

BAR QUILTS

Treating the Feathered Stars as unit blocks, where a square contains the whole star design, is natural for today's quilters. We are accustomed to designing our quilts with square units. Repeated close inspection of old Feathered Star quilts, however, shows that old-time quilters thought of the design quite differently. Most old Feathered Star quilts were not constructed block by block, but as bar quilts. Often called Joining or Touching Stars, the star centers and points were constructed as separate sections, then joined together in rows. Only when all the rows were joined would the star motifs emerge. The points of the stars touched each other, but unlike adjacent sets of whole-star blocks, the large squares between were without seam lines. The advantage was, of course, that spaces without seams allow for finer quilting. It is characteristic of the older Feathered Star quilts for these spaces to include lavish quilting, made easier and more attractive by bar construction, rather than block by block construction.

Some Feathered Star blocks are better suited to bar construction that others. In some, the units are simple, the seam lines straight. In others, construction requires set-in seams and halfway seams at every turn. If you intend to make a bar quilt from a Feathered Star block, choose a straightforward one with long seam construction.

To change any Feathered Star block design to bar quilt construction, double the large side triangle to make a square and quadruple the corner square to make a larger square. If you are in doubt as to how the pieces will fit, draw four Feathered Star blocks together. Erase the old unit block boundaries and identify the new units of construction.

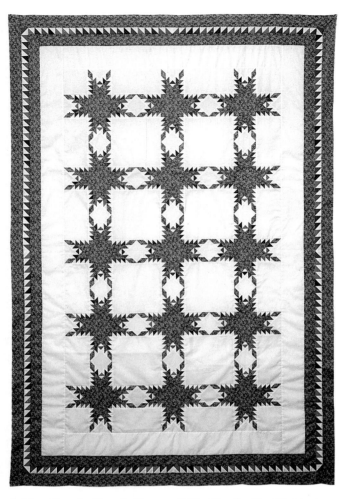

Joining Stars by Beverly Bynum, 1986, Woodinville, Washington, 71" x 102". This quilt top was constructed as a bar quilt from the Joining Star pattern that appears on page 77. Eighteen different blue fabrics were used for the feathers and sawtooth border. (Collection of the artist)

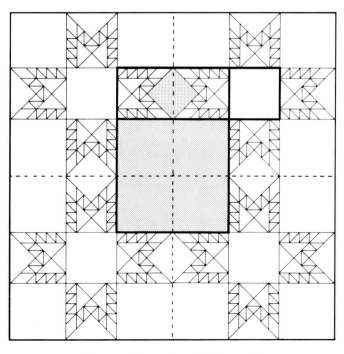

Construction units of a bar quilt

Feathered Star by one of three Hubbard sisters, c. 1860, Bastrop County, Texas, 80" x 97". Clearly taking advantage of bar construction, the maker of this quilt filled the counterpane areas with perfectly executed double clamshell quilting. The Flying Geese border carefully repeats the sawtooth motif in the stars. (From *Lone Stars: A Legacy of Texas Quilts, 1836-1936* by Karoline Patterson Bresenhan and Nancy O'Bryant Puentes, Copyright © 1986. Courtesy of the University of Texas Press. Owned by Barbara Leigh Rees)

BORDERS

Sawtooth borders are most commonly used on Feathered Star quilts because they echo the triangles edging the stars. More complex Delectable Mountains and Pineapple borders with their sawtooth edges also appear, as well as Streak of Lightning, Flying Geese, and other simple pieced borders. Most notable among borders used for Feathered Star quilts are the elaborately appliqued organic motifs, such as feather plumes, swags with bows, pineapples, vines, flowers, and trees. These flowing and curving border treatments appeared in contrast and balance to the geometric Feathered Stars, lending grace and elegance to the quilts.

Several quilt researchers have found the blue and white Feathered Star quilts with tree borders particularly interesting. Two are pictured here. It is easy when confronted with two such similar quilts to assume some sort of personal connection between the makers. Indeed, the strikingly similar quilts on page 52 and 53 were actually by the same maker, though found in different parts of the country.

But, the two blue and white quilts here, one from a New York collection and the other a family quilt from Kansas, have the look of early indigo and white woven coverlets, which were primarily produced in the northeastern United States. Many woven coverlets had oak tree or rosebush borders similar in configuration to the borders on these two quilts, though the trees in Patty Boyer's quilt look like willow trees — a symbol of mourning in 19th-century iconography.

Tree borders similar to these were part of the design vocabulary of weavers and quiltmakers of the time. Given the previous and concurrent design tradition in woven coverlets, we could assume that these two quilts were made independently of each other. The makers had similar design restrictions of color and motifs and lived in a time when such border imagery was common.

Feathered Star by Mary Elizabeth Togers Harvey, c. 1855-1875, Lewisburg, Pennsylvania, 64'' x 72''. The willow tree border on this quilt could mean that it was made to be a mourning quilt. It is strikingly similar to the quilt pictured on page 31 and was made by the great-great grandmother of the present owner. (Patricia L. Boyer, Lawrence, Kansas)

Feathered Star within Feathered Star, maker unknown, c. 1860, 98" x 82". The bold "trees" in the border, similar to those found in woven coverlets of the time, provide a strong frame for the intricate central design. (Private collection. Photo courtesy of American Hurrah Antiques and E. P. Dutton, Inc.)

Feathered Stars, maker unknown, 1856, Michigan, 97'' x 99''. Worn but still lovely, this red, green, and white Feathered Star quilt, with the unusual combination of pieced peonies and appliqued stems and leaves in the border, was justifiably a source of pride for its makers. Pieced as a bar quilt to accommodate fine quilting, it is initialed and dated in nine white squares with nine different sets of initials. The counterpanes are quilted with varying motifs. One includes interlocking rings and a heart, possibly indicating that this is a bride's quilt. (Nancy Sheafe, Tigard, Oregon)

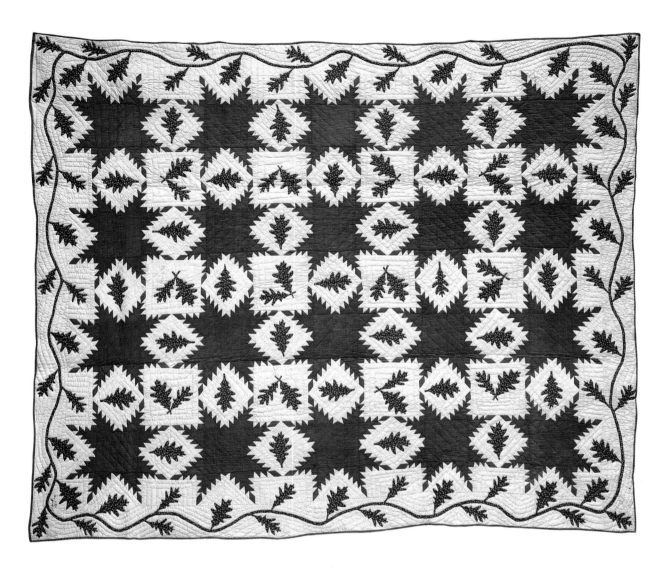

Feathered Star with Oak Leaf by Mary A. Purdy, 1869, New York, 82'' x 91''. A winding green calico border with evenly spaced oak leaves frames 20 red Feathered Stars that alternate with white squares appliqued with oak leaves. The print used for the applique is a triple leaf in yellow and green on a black background. The quilt is bound with the red fabric and backed with coarse cotton. The batt is light with few cotton seeds. In one corner is penned in black ink: "Mary A. Purdy, June 18, 1869." (Photo courtesy of the Shelburne Museum, Shelburne, Vermont)

Feathered Star or **Sawtooth** by Marietta Pierce, c. 1840-1845, Matildaville, New York, 64½'' x 83½''. Marietta Pierce probably made this quilt shortly before her marriage to Loyson Moses Stow in 1846. She used the Feathered Star as a border motif around three sides. The green textile was formed by first dyeing the cloth yellow and then overdyeing with blue. The fugitive green has disappeared in places due to washing and exposure to light. (Photo courtesy of the DAR Museum, Washington, D.C., Acc. no. 62.27)

HISTORY

Women's art and home crafts traditionally have not been well documented, so searching for definite origins of a particular patchwork design like the Feathered Star is bound to end in frustration. The available records are museum files and the published and unpublished findings of other quilt researchers. Best are the quilts themselves, sometimes documented, but most times not. Workmanship, textiles, and size can tell us some things, but a lack of definitive written sources leaves much to conjecture and interpretation.

The Feathered Star probably evolved from other quilt patterns. Perhaps the creation of the design was an expression of thrift, a pattern made to use up small bits of fabric. The *Kansas City Star* in 1935 encouraged quilters to make a Feathered Star quilt for just this reason: "Dark and light scraps of the smallest and most irregular size may be used in the Pine Cone quilt."

Ruth Finley, in 1929, in *Old Patchwork Quilts and the Women Who Made Them*, described pieced quilt designs:

> "Another great favorite was the 'Rising Star.' . . . This ancient pattern was the inspiration for many designs more elaborate, one of the most successful being 'The Feathered Star.'"

The Rising Star, like many Feathered Star designs, is based on a simple sawtooth star.

Another speculation on the origin of this intricate and beautiful design first appeared in *Woman's Day Magazine* in 1941:

> An old variation of the Lemon Star is the Feathered Star. There is an old design that came to America in crewel work and became an applique pattern in the South; it is called the Princess Feather. The English took it from the three feather crest of the Prince of Wales. No one knows the origin of the Feathered Star, this is only a guess. But the Feathered Star looks as if a woman, thinking of the Prince's Feather, thoughtfully cut out triangles and gave a feathery edge to her enlarged Lemon Star. [2]

Although the argument sounds convincing, comparison of the patterns shows clearly that the geometric Lemon Star and Feathered Star are similar to each other, and completely different from the original flowing Princess Feather.

Princess Feather by Sarah Lhamon, 1861, Mt. Vernon, Ohio. The Princess Feather was a very popular pattern after 1850. Many examples of the design were made in the red and green fabrics then in fashion. The design can be traced to the feather crest of the English Prince of Wales and has been worked in quilting and crewel as well as in applique. This quilt is signed and dated in the center. (Collection of That Patchwork Place, Inc., Bothell, Washington)

2. *Rose Wilder Lane, Woman's Day Book of American Needlework* p. 84.

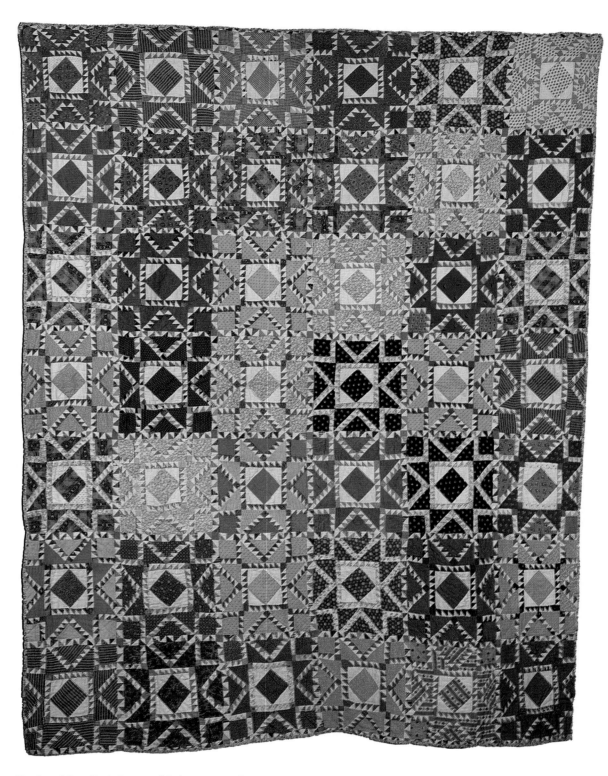

Feathered Star Variation possibly by Mrs. Davis Layton,c. 1815-1830, location unknown, 81'' x 71''. ''Mrs. Davis Layton'' is stamped on this quilt, which possibly indicates she was the maker. Relying on the fabrics used, several quilt historians agreed upon the years 1815-1830 (very early for a Feathered Star design), for the date of this quilt. (Photo courtesy of the Oregon Historical Society, Portland, Oregon, OHS 62-377)

Some Feathered Star designs look as if their sawtooth edges could have been influenced by the decorative art of native American women, as suggested by Patricia Mainardi in her essay, "Quilts, the Great American Art":

> Early American immigrants came from England, Ireland, Germany, and the Netherlands and mingled the needlework traditions of those countries. In America, they met with new design traditions from the various American Indian tribes whose influence is obvious in the many quilts named for them: Indian Meadow, Indian Hatchet, Indian Trails to name a few. The familiar sawtooth pattern, for example, seen in both pieced and applique quilts is strikingly similar to Indian women's weaving. Furthermore, intermarriage between Indian women and white men was fairly common, and the Indian women and their female descendants' quilts would bring together design influences from both cultures. [3]

Which Indian Groups could have influenced quilters and what did their art look like? Many books on Indian crafts acknowledge the European influence on Indian designs, but seem to ignore the possibility that influence could have flowed the other way.

Very early patterns for patchwork offered in magazines and catalogs in the 1800s gave only pictures of designs. Quilters were expected to devise and make their own templates. Women learned early the geometries of pieced work, and if a pattern could not be worked out, a "more mathematically inclined" male could probably be found to help with the task.

Florence Peto, in *Historic Quilts,* suggests that traveling peddlers "alert to the needs of housewives" could have been the "carriers of quilt patterns that appeared over so wide a radius of territory at approximately the same time." [4] Because so many Feathered Star quilts are strikingly similar, it is easy to assume that the makers were in some way connected, whether by family, physical proximity, the regular circuit of a peddler, or subscription to the same magazines.

Jonathan Holstein in *The Pieced Quilt, An American Design Tradition,* talks of the creation of patchwork designs:

> The women who made functional quilts — and made up the patterns — were largely unschooled, and certainly not trained in geometry. Yet they, and perhaps their husbands, had a practical knowledge of design that they used in their daily work . . . . I have found a few indications that some quilt patterns may have been designed by country farmer-builders for their wives; their practical knowledge of geometry would have been of much use in such an endeavor. However, it is my feeling that the great majority of these patterns were designed by women who exploited the simple divisions and arrangements of the square. [5]

An intricate geometric pattern like the Feathered Star obviously was within the conceptual abilities of 19th-century quiltmakers, because Feathered Star quilts were made. But who first edged her star with little triangles and called them feathers? There must have been a first Feathered Star quilt. The variety of feathered designs suggests numerous design sources and ingenuity on the part of many quilters. The first

Feathered Star quilts were admired and copied by other quilters. Most likely design changes were made by each subsequent quilter until the original quiltmaker and her quilt became forgotten — anonymous.

Not only did women copy patterns, they openly shared then. Alice Morse Earle in *Home Life in Colonial Days* wrote:

> Women revelled in intricate and difficult patchwork; they eagerly exchanged patterns with one another; they talked over designs and admired pretty bits of calico and pondered combinations to make. [6]

Most of the Feathered Star quilts in collections today seem to have been made in the last three-quarters of the 19th century in the more settled parts of the United States. Quilts found on the West Coast rarely were made there, but were brought from the East and Midwest.

Several Feathered Star quilts are tentatively dated as early as 1835. One quilt from the collection of the Oregon Historical Society has been reliably dated by written account and by the fabrics used to 1815-1830.

Though most Feathered Star quilts were made between 1850 and 1900, perhaps not all were made in America. Examples of Feathered Star quilts dating concurrently with American quilts are found in catalogs of Irish quilts. And the unusual green and red Feathered Star variation pictured here is, by family account, from Scotland.

Radiant Star Christmas Banner by Marsha McCloskey, 1986, Seattle, Washington, 23" x 54". Instructions for this small Feathered Star project begin on page 110. (Collection of the author. Photo courtesy of *Quilter's Newsletter Magazine*)

3. *Patricia Mainardi, Quilts, the Great American Art,* pp. 16 - 17.

4. *Florence Peto, Historic Quilts*, p. XVII.

5. *Jonathan Holstein, The Pieced Quilt, An American Design Tradition,* p. 56.

6. *Alice Morse Earle, Home Life in Colonial Days,* p. 271.

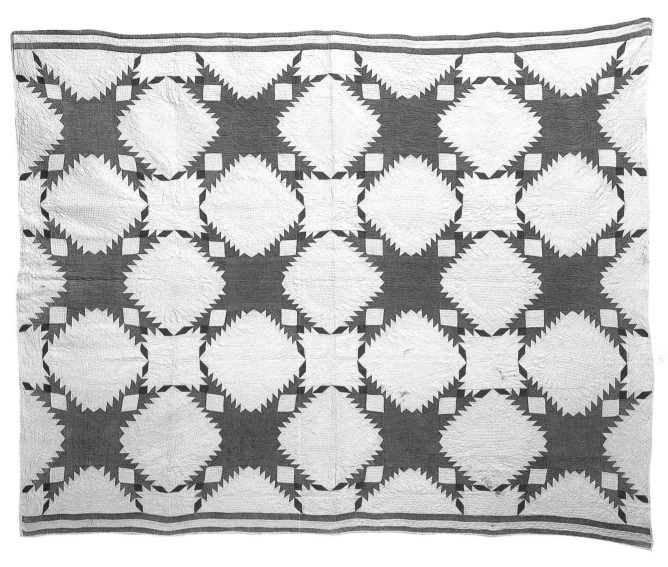

Antique Star by Mrs. Gilray, 1833, Scotland, 72" x 88". This exceptional red, green, and white Feathered Star variation is a family quilt passed through several generations. The letter of transmittal for this quilt reads:

July 1st —

Grandmother Gilray made this quilt when she was a girl in Scotland. We do not know how old she was, but her first baby was born in 1836 so am assuming this quilt was made in 1833. When Grandmother died the quilt went to Mother Youmans and then in 1910 when Mother died I got the quilt so it is at least one hundred and four years old . . . and now in 1937 I am giving it to Marie Youmans.

Minnie Bawtinheimer
Parma, Idaho

(Grace Bawtinheimer, Arlington, Washington)

Radiant Star Christmas Quilt by Phyllis Saelens, 1986, Seattle, Washington, 74" x 74". This quilt was made using the 15" Radiant Star pattern that appears on page 92. The same pattern in a 12" size was available from Aunt Martha's catalog in the 1930s. (Collection of the artist)

38

Another group of Feathered Star quilts was made during the quilt revival of the early 20th century, when quilting was generally encouraged as a thrifty and patriotic activity. At that time, old patterns were retrieved and widely published.

During the 1920s and 1930s the *Kansas City Star, Hearth and Home,* and the *Ladies Home Journal* were among publications offering Feathered Star patterns. A pattern for a 12'' Radiant Star or Chestnut Burr was offered through Aunt Martha's Catalog in the 1930s. And the Ladies Art Company in St. Louis, Missouri, offered three Feathered Star variations as early as 1897. Feathered Star quilts from this era can sometimes be matched with published patterns.

The advertisement reproduced here is from a pattern brochure, *Household's Quilt Block Service,* from Household Supplies in Topeka, Kansas. The yellow and white color combination suggested for their Star of Bethlehem was used often in 20th century quilts. One that I know of, dated 1941, is in a quilt collection in Des Moines, Iowa. Another, of the same pattern but called the World's Fair Quilt or Golden Splendor, is in a collection of Tennessee quilts. It was exhibited as the Philadelphia Fair in 1926 after being judged through a national county fair contest the "best quilt in all the 48 states and U.S. Territories."[7]

There is a surge of interest in the Feathered Star design now, too, and more and more contemporary quilters are working the intricate blocks. The current quilt revival is maturing, and new quilters who once were satisfied with simpler designs are now seeking greater challenges in their needlework. The Feathered Star pattern, with its intricate look and opportunities for fine quilting, provides such a challenge.

7. *Quilter's Newsletter Magazine, no. 190 (March, 1987), p. 6.*

Star of Bethlehem Inspires Quilters

Early American women who went a-quilting found inspiration for patterns in the simple surroundings of their everyday lives, in the beauties of nature and their own religious thoughts. One of the choice quilt designs to come down thru the generations is The Star of Bethlehem.

A Star of Bethlehem quilt made of gold and w h i t e will light up a bedroom as the star lighted the pathway to the obscure manger long ago. Our actual-size quilt pattern simplifies the work. The quilting design used for the plain blocks goes over the entire square, with no need for fastening of thread until the entire design is completed. It is an additional 15 cents.

Advertisement for Feathered Star pattern. Household Supplies, Topeka, Kansas.

The World's Fair Quilt by Lillian Jackson Jones, 1923-24, Givson County, Tennessee, 74¼'' x 95½''. Mrs. Jones made fine quilts because she "wasn't very pretty, so I had to have something to show for myself." After her success with this quilt, she gave up quilts for afghans and politics. (Robert B. Hicks, III. Photo courtesy of Bets Ramsey and Merikay Waldvogel, authors of *The Quilts of Tennessee.*)

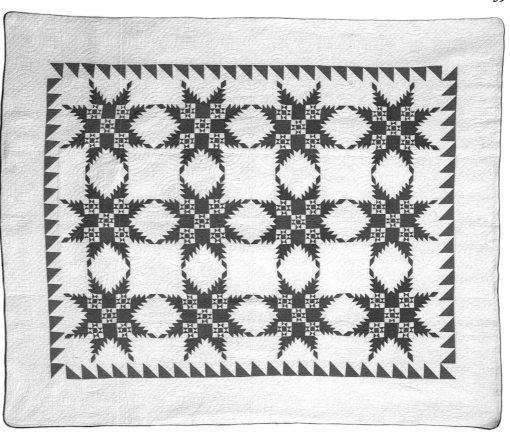

California Star by Gertrude Dobbins Jackson, c. 1935, Wolcott, Indiana, 83'' x 100''. Gertrude Jackson and her husband, Bert Jackson, were of pioneer stock that settled in Indiana in the late 1860s. Many of Gertrude's quilts were pieced of 1930s fabrics, and this fine example of the California Star pattern is the same as the one in Carrie Hall's *The Romance of the Patchwork Quilt,* published in 1935. (James and Barbara Rickey, Bellevue, Washington)

Rob's Star by Louise Kindig, 1986, Brookings, Oregon, 63'' x 81''. In designing this Radiant Star quilt, the maker was assisted by her son, Rob. The quilt is named for him. (Collection of the artist)

Feathered Star, origin unknown, c. 1880, 70'' x 76½''. In sharp contrast to formal two-color Feathered Star quilts, this scrappy interpretation takes your breath away. Audacious use of fabrics tells of a quiltmaker with unusual disregard for tradition, or perhaps a woman doing the absolute best she could with available fabrics. (Lindsay Horton, Seattle, Washington)

Feathered Star, maker unknown, Marshalltown, Iowa, c. 1900, 65'' x 86''. Plaid background fabric and an assortment of scraps were combined to make this satisfying quilt. (Judy Mathieson, Woodland Hills, California)

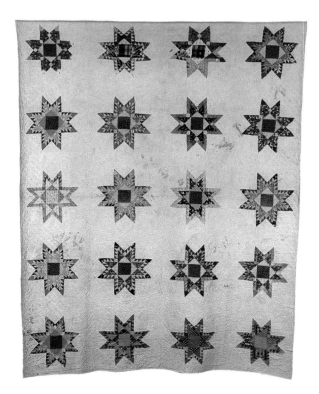

Feathered Star or **Sawtooth,** maker unknown, c. 1870-1880, possibly southern United States, 72'' x 80''. This delightful scrap Feathered Star is enlivened by the quilter's alternation of dark and light triangles, which in some stars create a feathered edge and in others a closed edge. Household remnants, including polychrome roller prints, dyed and white cottons, plaid wools, and linens have been used in the piecing. The backing is blue and white plaid linen. (Photo courtesy of the DAR Museum, Washington, D.C., Acc. no. 70202)

Feathered Star Variation, origin unknown, c. 1870, 69'' x 87''. Twenty stars made of scraps are set on-point, with alternate plain squares that accommodate a fine quilting pattern. (Photo courtesy of the Oregon Historical Society, Portland, Oregon, OHS 72-94.11)

Monroe Family Feathered Star Quilt, c. 1900, Kansas, 64″ x 90″. This quilt belonged to a prominent pioneer family in the Kansas Territory. Lilla Day came with her parents to Kansas from Indiana in 1884. She married a young lawyer, Lee Monroe, who became a respected judge. An early feminist, Lilla also became a lawyer and founded two publications that worked for women's rights and better living and working conditions. Her collection of 800 personal histories of early Kansas pioneer women lead eventually to the publication of *Pioneer Women, Voices from the Kansas Frontier*, a book written by her great-granddaughter Joanna Stratton.

Twenty-one pink and brown print Star of Chamblie blocks are set alternately with unpieced squares embellished with appliqued six-pointed stars. Tiny triangles complete the Delectable Mountains borders. The backing is turned to the front in a ¼″ hem for the edge finish. (Valerie Vallaas, Wenatchee, Washington)

Twinkling Star by Marsha McCloskey, 1986, Seattle, Washington, 26'' x 26''. This doll or wall quilt was inspired by the Twinkling Star quilt from the Oregon Historical Society. The pattern and instructions for this small Feathered Star project are on page 107. (Collection of the author)

Twinkling Star by Martha Ardella Hodson, c. 1880, Kansas, 60'' x 85½''. This quilt inspired the author to make the small pastel Twinkling Star quilt pictured here. Martha Ardella Hodson married Thomas Edward Ratcliff near Northbranch, Jewell County, Kansas. The family traveled west over the Oregon Trail in 1895. (Photo courtesy of the Oregon Historical Society, Portland, Oregon, OHS 63-58)

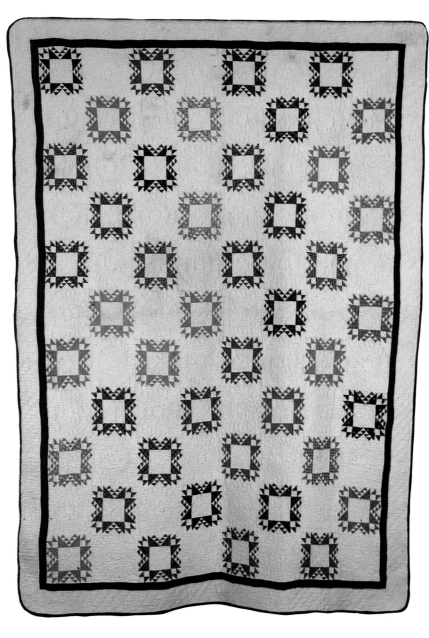

PRESTIGE THROUGH QUILTING

Competition among quiltmakers has been acknowledged for a long time and should be regarded as healthy for both the quiltmakers and their art form. Nineteenth-century women were tied by convention and necessity to their homes. Quilting was one of the acceptable activities that led out of that isolation. It brought them to quilting bees, where they shared patterns and fabrics, as well as news, advice, and gossip. Needlework could also give a woman a chance to shine publicly, to gain status in community circles. Difficult quilt patterns, such as the Feathered Star, served as benchmarks of achievement and a way for women to feel pride and accomplishment.

Patricia Mainardi comments on the special care given to their "best" quilts:

> Moreover, the women who made quilts knew and valued what they were doing: frequently quilts were signed and dated by the maker, listed in her will with specific instructions as to who should inherit them, and treated with all the care that a fine piece of art deserves. Women reserved their "best" quilt for guests of honor or special occasions, and when it was on the bed drew the curtains to prevent fading. Many of the most beautiful quilts were actually used so infrequently that they have come down to us without ever having been laundered. Women even made special "quilt cases" to store them in. Even in their choice of material, women quiltmakers behaved similarly to other artists. They wanted to use only the most permanent materials, and the popularity of two colors, indigo and turkey red (an alizarin dye), was the result of their ability to withstand much use without fading. [8]

Indigo dye made a durable blue, well known by quilters for its fastness. Hundreds of dark indigo blue prints were produced commercially during the 19th century, and blue and white quilts were produced in abundance. This classic color combination is probably the one most commonly found in feathered star quilts from this period.

Gail Binney-Winslow, in *Homage to Amanda,* comments on the competitive spirit and blue and white quilts:

> During the second half of the nineteenth century, blue-and-white quilts . . . attained status among quiltmakers, or those aspiring to high standards. They became repositories of fine stitchery, and it is within their borders that we see virtuoso quilting. [9]

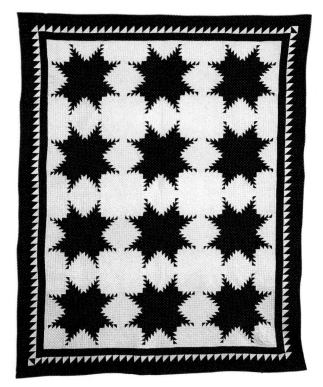

Feathered Star, origin unknown, 1885, 81" x 63". Embroidered in one corner of this classic blue and white Feathered Star quilt is "Aunt Lil to Daisy, 1885." (Bryce and Donna Hamilton, Minneapolis, Minnesota)

8. Patricia Mainardi, QUILTS, THE GREAT AMERICAN ART, p. 6.
9. Gail Binney-Winslow, HOMAGE TO AMANDA, p. 85.

Feathered Star with Sunburst Center, maker unknown, Missouri, c. 1880-1885, 88'' x 90''. In this classic blue and white Feathered Star, the circular center sunbursts stand out and determine the quilt's visual character. (Karey P. Bresenhan, Houston, Texas)

Feathered Star, origin unknown, top c. 1890, 82'' x 71''. Found by the owner as a top at a flea market in Portland, Oregon, this blue and white Feathered Star was quilted by Ruby Dicken in the late 1970s. (Nancy Sheafe, Tigard, Oregon)

Feathered Star by Ollie and Lydia McNiel, c. 1925, Berryville, Arkansas, 72'' x 81''. Two sisters pieced this blue and white Feathered Star quilt by hand. It was quilted by their aunt, Mrs. Golda Jones of Ozark, Missouri, in the late 1940s. Notice the unusual pieced lattice cornerstones. (Jan Halgrimson, Edmonds, Washington)

Feathered Star by the Austin Area Quilt Guild, 1984, Austin, Texas, 96'' x 100''. Made as a donation quilt, this is a reproduction of an 1851 Feathered Star quilt that appeared in *Lady's Circle Patchwork* magazine in 1979. Some 121 guild members and 13 guests worked on this quilt, producing it over two weeks at a quilting bee planned by Kathleen McCrady. It is hand-pieced and hand-quilted and took a total of approximately 615 hours to make. (Owned by Carmen Beyer. Photo courtesy of the Austin Area Quilt Guild)

Feathered Star with Zigzag Border, maker unknown, c. 1880, Ohio, 71'' x 75''. (Franklin and Mary Daenzer. Photo courtesy of the East Bay Heritage Quilters)

Feathered Star by Imogene Gooch, 1983, Rockville, Indiana, 81'' x 96''. Made from pattern No. 32 of the Mountain Mist series, this quilt won an Honorable Mention in the 1983 Mountain Mist Quilt Contest. (Photo courtesy of the Stearns Technical Textiles Company)

Feathered Star, maker unknown, Ohio, c. 1875-1890, 72'' x 72''. Small scale and fine quilting combine to make this a very lovely two-color design. (Karey P. Bresenhan, Houston, Texas)

Double Feathered Star with Lightning Streak Border, maker unknown, Michigan, c. 1845, 88'' x 88''. An unusual scale change between the inner and outer stars gives this quilt a unique visual emphasis. (Roger and Keiko Keyes. Photo courtesy of the East Bay Heritage Quilters)

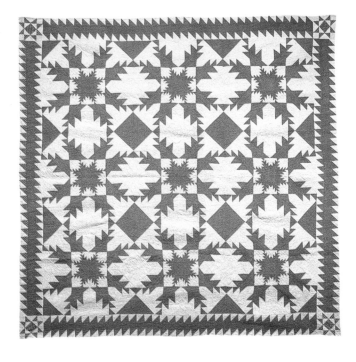

Feathered Star, maker unknown, Ohio, c. 1880-1890, 91½'' x 89''. Though double Feathered Stars are occasionally found, this triple Feathered Star is extremely rare. Wonderful embroidery fills the negative spaces, where other quilters most often have depended on quilting motifs. (Collection of Sandra Mitchell. This quilt first appeared in *The Quilt Digest 3,* published by The Quilt Digest Press, San Francisco. Photo courtesy of the publisher.)

LOOK-ALIKE QUILTS

The Feathered Star was often worked in blue and white, and the quilts often have lavish quilting. But virtuoso quilting on Feathered Star quilts is not limited to blue and white examples. For instance, in the red and white Feathered Star quilt from the Museum of History and Industry in Seattle, the stars themselves are poorly pieced, but the quilting, stuffed work, and trapunto are top quality. The quilt was made by the Tingle sisters, and their initials are worked in trapunto in the center of each side border. Under the initials L. T., a small heart is worked into the quilting, leading to the belief that it was a wedding quilt made for Lucretia Tingle. A cloth label on the back is printed by the donor, Fannie Scott Bent. It reads:

> Evelyn Tingle was one of four sisters who made this quilt. She was a young lady in 1825, so the quilt may be 132 years old now — 1957. My mother was Margaret Tingle, a niece of these sisters and the quilt was given to her.

Another in the series of look-alike quilts, the Tingle quilt — except for its sawtooth borders — is nearly identical to a quilt from the collection of The Warren County Historical Society in Ohio. Pictured in *Ohio Quilts, A Living Tradition,* the caption with the quilt reads:

> Feathered Star. c. 1850. Waynesville, Warren County. 95" x 95". The Hunt family came from South Carolina to establish Keldere Farm near Waynesville in 1805. A member of the family was responsible for this outstanding example of stuffed quilting. [10]

The research trail begins here. Were the Hunts and Tingles related? Why are the two quilts so much alike? The quilts are similar in color, block pattern, number of blocks, sets, feather wreaths, and plumes quilted in the alternate blocks, along with distinctive urn-and-feather stuffed work in the borders. The connection could have been, as noted earlier in the discussion of pattern sources, a traveling peddler, close proximity, or subscriptions to the same periodicals.

Feathered Star by a member of the Hunt family, c. 1850, Waynesville, Warren County, Ohio, 92" x 95". The stuffed work in this quilt and in the Tingle quilt is remarkable, particularly the broad borders with the classic urns framed by flowers and wreaths. All aspects of both quilts combine to indicate that they were treasured family heirlooms and that they are in some way related. (Warren County Historical Society. Photo courtesy of E. P. Dutton, Inc.)

10. Canton Art Institute, OHIO QUILTS, A LIVING TRADITION, p. 15.

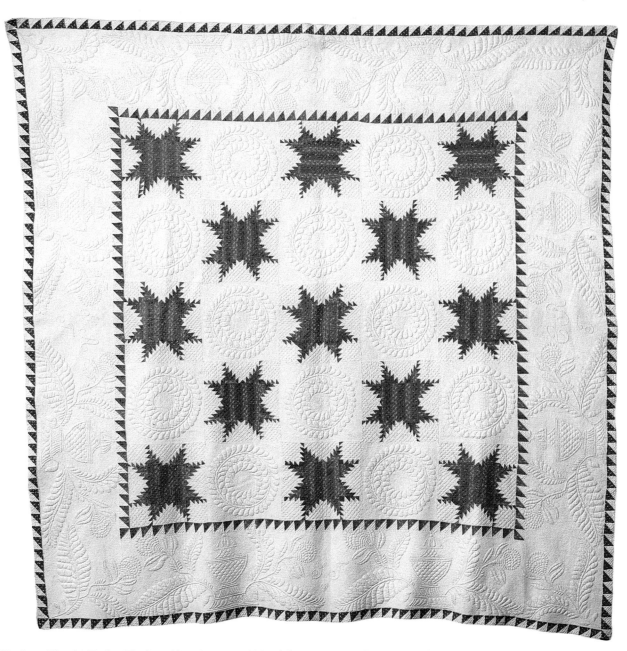

Feathered Star by Evelyn Tingle and her sisters, c. 1825, origin unknown, 84" x 96". Possibly made as a wedding quilt for Lucretia Tingle, this quilt is amazingly similar to the Hunt family quilt from Ohio. (Photo courtesy of the Museum of History and Industry, Seattle, Washington.)

Another set of look-alike quilts is the pair made by Nancy Bogart Hasford in Geneva, New York around 1865. Mrs. Hasford was born in 1815 and died in 1892. The first of her two quilts was documented during a quilt search (A Common Thread . . . Quilting in the Yakima Valley) sponsored by the Yakima Valley Museum and Historical Society. This quilt was brought to the Yakima Valley in Washington State in 1910 by Alida Pierce and has stayed in the original family. The second quilt was collected in New York State and is now in the collection of American Hurrah Antiques in New York City. Both quilts are outstanding examples of American quilt and folk art. The main difference between them is the central motif. As examples of Feathered Star quilts, they are highly unusual because of the applique wreaths surrounding each star.

Flower Wreath and Stars by Nancy Bogart Hasford, c. 1865, Geneva New York, 76" x 85½". This quilt was brought to the Yakima Valley in Washington State in 1910 by Alida Pierce and has stayed in the original family. (Owned by Jean Tracy. Photo courtesy of the Yakima Valley Museum and Historical Society).

Feathered Star and Wreath by Nancy Bogart Hasford, c. 1865, Geneva, New York, 77'' x 75''. Nancy Bogart Hasford apparently enjoyed this pattern very much. She made both quilts pictured here. This quilt was collected in New York State. The main difference in the quilts is the central motif. Otherwise nearly identical, both are outstanding examples of American Folk Art. (Photo courtesy of American Hurrah Antiques, New York, New York)

PIECING FEATHERED STAR BLOCKS

Templates and piecing instructions for twenty different Feathered Star blocks can be found in the pattern section of this book. The blocks range in size from 10" to 28". Over thirty block variations are possible, using the templates given. You can further multiply the possibilities by changing color arrangements.

All the Feathered Star blocks can be pieced on the sewing machine. Before you start, read the following general tips on machine piecing, then go on to the individual patterns and the cutting and piecing diagrams provided.

Star Spangled Banner block by Marsha McCloskey, 1983, Seattle, Washington, 28" x 28". This block is the most intricate of the Feathered Star designs. It contains over 600 pieces. The pattern for this block is on page 66. (Collection of the author)

COLOR

Visually, the most important parts of the star are the center and the points. Placing an important color such as red in both places will set up a relationship that will draw your eye from one to the other. An example of this type of color placement is the Radiant Star on page 9.

The feathers, too, are important in these stars. The two fabrics chosen for feathers should have good contrast, a light and a dark fabric. It is a good place to use solids or more solid-looking prints. Make sure that both the feathers and points stand out clearly from the background fabric.

Choose good quality, lightweight, closely woven, 100 percent cotton fabrics for your Feathered Stars. Polyester content may make small patchwork pieces difficult to cut and sew accurately. Preshrink all fabrics before use. Wash light and dark colors separately with regular laundry detergent and warm water. If you suspect a dark color might run, rinse it separately in plain warm water until the water remains clear. Dry fabrics in the dryer and press them well before cutting.

TEMPLATES

Templates in the pattern section are grouped to save space. The instructions for each Feathered Star block will tell which templates to use and where to find them.

Each Feathered Star block diagram is accompanied by a list of the number of pieces to cut of each color. An "R" in the cutting notations means "reverse." These pieces (often the points of the star) are mirror images. Cut the first number of pieces with the template face up, then flip it over and cut the remaining pieces with the template face down.

1. Reproduce pattern pieces on paper. Roughly cut the paper pattern pieces (outside the cutting line). Glue each paper pattern to a thin piece of plastic (X-ray film is good) or posterboard. Then cut out the paper pattern and its stiffening together, exactly on the cutting line.

2. Study the design and templates. Decide on fabric and color arrangement. Determine the number of pieces to cut of each template and each fabric.

3. Press and fold fabric so that two pieces can be cut at one time (except linear designs which must be cut one at a time). Position the template on the fabric so that the arrows match the straight of grain. With a sharp pencil (white for dark fabrics, lead for light ones), trace around the template. The mark on the fabric is the cutting line. Using sharp fabric scissors, cut just inside this line to most accurately duplicate the template.

Chain piecing

 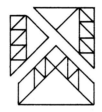

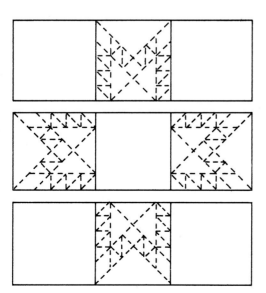

MACHINE PIECING

1. Sew exact 1/4" seams. To determine the 1/4" seam allowance on your machine, place a template under the presser foot and gently lower the needle onto the seam line. The distance from the needle to the edge of the template is 1/4". Some presser feet are exactly 1/4" wide and can be used as a seam guide. If the presser foot is narrower or wider, place a piece of masking tape at the edge of the template to act as a 1/4" guide.

2. In general, for straight seam piecing, sew from cut edge to cut edge. Backstitch if you wish, although it is not necessary as each seam will be crossed and held by another. Exceptions will be noted.

3. Stitch length should be set at 10 to 12 stitches per inch.

4. Use chain piecing whenever possible to save time and thread. To chain piece, sew one seam, but do not lift the presser foot. Do not take the piece out of the sewing machine and do not cut the thread. Instead, set up the next seam to be sewn and stitch it as you did the first. There will be a little twist of thread between the pieces. Sew all the seams you can at one time, then remove the "chain" and clip the threads.

5. Sew the smallest pieces together first to form units. Join small units to form larger ones until the block is complete. Refer frequently to the design diagrams and sewing instructions.

6. Short seams need not be pinned unless matching is involved or the seam is more than 4" long. Keep pins away from the seam line. Sewing over pins makes it hard to be accurate in tight places and tends to burr the needle.

Pressing

To produce a nice, flat star and to distribute the bulk of so many seam allowances, press seams open on the rows of feather triangles. Start by pressing the seams open on the bias-strip piecing and continue as the feather units are joined together. Other seams in the blocks should pressed to one side, in whichever direction they seem to fall. When there is a choice, press toward the darker fabric. Avoid excess ironing as you sew because it tends to stretch biases and distort fabric shapes.

Bias-Strip Piecing

To me, bias-strip piecing is the most important part of piecing Feathered Stars. Without it, I simply would not have the patience to complete many blocks. It is an accurate and fast method for piecing the numerous, small half-square triangles that are the "feathers" in all the Feathered Star patterns.

The basic method is presented here. Many quilters have adapted the concept to other shapes and even to rotary cutting. Consider bias-strip piecing for any shape consisting of two equal triangles. The split-diamond points on the Sitka Rose block pictured on page 57 were pieced using bias strips and a diamond template.

To cut enough feathers from bias-strips for an average Feathered Star block, cut two 14" to 18" squares, one of each fabric used for the feather units. Layer the two squares, mark the top layer as shown, and cut both at the same time. Nearly all the feathers in the patterns in this book can be made with 2" wide strips. To determine the width of bias strips for other projects, measure the square template to be used diagonally corner to corner (including seam allowances). Add 3" and divide by two.

$$\frac{X'' + 3''}{2} = \text{width of each bias strip}$$

Sew the strips together on the long bias edge, using 1/4" seam allowance. Press seams open. Place a stiffened square template on the right side of the bias-strip unit, lining up opposite corners with the seam line. Trace around the template. Start at one end and make a string of squares the length of the seam line. Carefully cut out the fabric squares, cutting only on the drawn lines (actually just inside the drawn lines). This will yield several squares made up of two triangles, with outside edges on the straight grain of the fabric. Two funny-shaped pieces will be left over. Seam the long straight edges of these together, press, and make another set of squares.

Half-square triangles

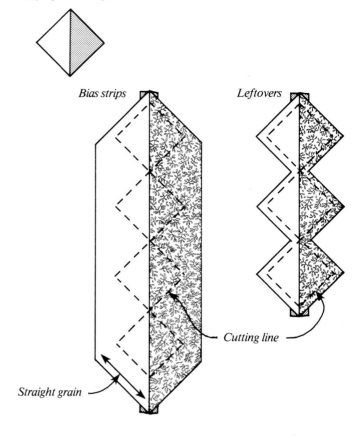

Bias strips   *Leftovers*

Cutting line

Straight grain

Quarter-square triangles   *Split diamonds*

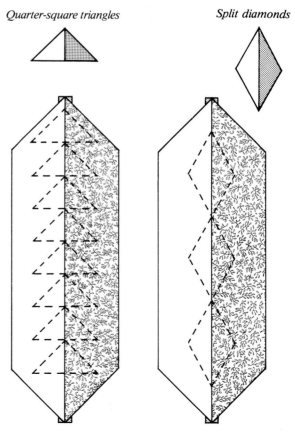

Consider using bias-strip piecing for any shape consisting of two equal triangles.

Making bias strips

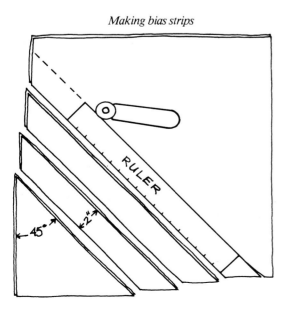

RULER

45°   2"

Matching Tips

Here are eight matching techniques that can be helpful in many different piecing situations.

1. Opposing Seams: When stitching one seamed unit to another, press seam allowances in opposite directions on seams that need to match. The two "opposing" seams will hold each other in place and evenly distribute the bulk. Plan pressing to take advantage of opposing seams.

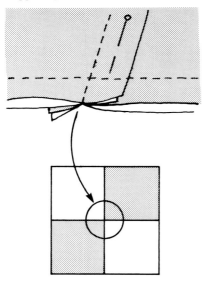

Opposing seams

Sitka Rose by Marsha McCloskey, 1984, Seattle, Washington, 24" x 24". No pattern. (Collection of the author)

2. Positioning Pin: A pin, carefully pushed straight through two points that need to match and pulled tight, will establish the proper point of matching. Pin the seam normally and remove the positioning pin before stitching.

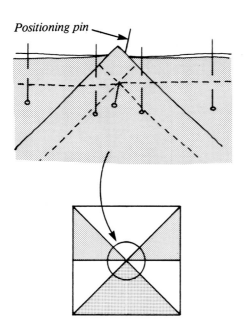

Positioning pin

3. The "X": When triangles are pieced, stitches will form an "X" at the next seamline. Stitch through the center of the "X" to make sure the points on the sewn triangles will not be chopped off.

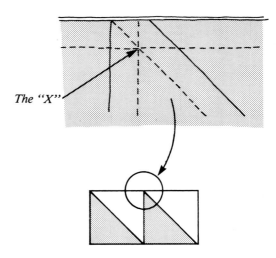

The "X"

When seams are pressed open on the rows of feathers, the "X" will look like this. Sew right through the point indicated for crisply pieced points. Sew with these seams on top so the "X" can be seen clearly.

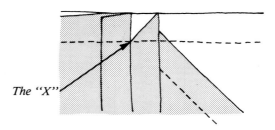

The "X"

4. Easing: When two pieces to be sewn together are supposed to match but instead are slightly different lengths, pin the points of matching and stitch with the shorter piece on top. The feed dog eases the fullness of the bottom piece.

5. Making Eight Points Come Together: To make eight points come together crisply, follow these three steps: First, chain-piece light and dark triangles together to form four squares. Press each seam toward the dark. Second, make two halves of the pinwheel by sewing two square units together as shown. Match, using opposing diagonal seams. Press each new seam toward the dark. Third, sew the center seam. Match, using positioning pin and opposing seams. Stitch exactly through the "X."

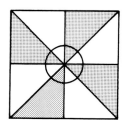

1.

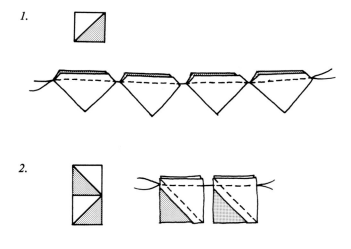

2.

3.

The "X"

6. Set-in Seams: Where three seam lines come together at an angle, stop all stitching at the 1/4'' seam line and backtack. Don't let even one stitch extend into the seam allowance. As each seam is finished, take the work out of the machine, position the next seam, and start stitching in the new direction. Backtacking is necessary because these seam lines will not be crossed and held by any other stitches.

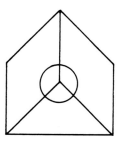

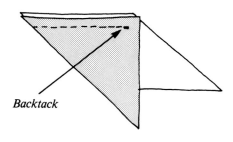

Backtack

7. Halfway Seams: In many Feathered Star blocks, halfway seams are used to complete the star points and avoid set-in seams. Certain seams, which will be indicated in the block piecing diagrams, are to be sewn halfway, early in block construction, and then completed in the last stages of sewing. Begin and end these lines of stitching with backtacking.

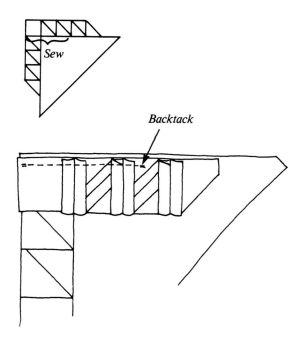

Sew

Backtack

8. Curved Seams: Only one pattern in this book involves curved seams. They can easily be sewn on the sewing machine. To help the concave curve stretch, carefully score it by making 1/16'' clips about 1/16'' apart along inner edge of curve. Match centers of the two pieces and pin as shown, carefully matching raw edges. Stitch with 1/4'' seam allowance.

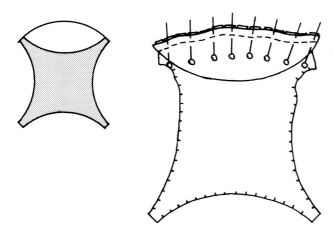

The Star System

If you glance through the following pattern section, you will notice that each Feathered Star pattern drawing has one, two, or three small stars next to it. These stars are a rating system to tell you how easy or difficult that block is to piece. One-star blocks are the simplest and three-star blocks are the most intricate.

* One star — very simple. These Feathered Star blocks involve only straight-seam piecing and the longest seams go all the way across the block.

** Two stars — simple. These blocks are really not much more involved than one-star blocks. The piecing is still all straight seams, but halfway seams are used to complete the points of the stars. In these blocks, the longest seams begin and end at points inside the block, and halfway seams are used to avoid set-in seams.

*** Three stars — complex. I find these blocks challenging. (But we all need a challenge now and then, right?) They contain straight seams, halfway seams, plus either set-in or curved seams or both. Hand piecers and skilled machine piecers will have no problems with these blocks.

One Star

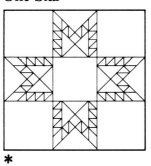
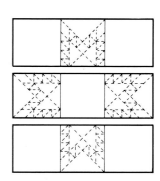

*

Two Stars

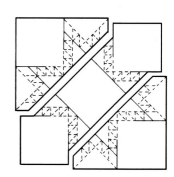

* *

Three Stars

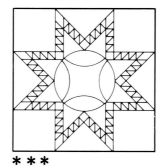
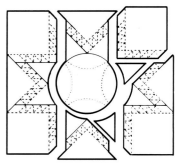

* * *

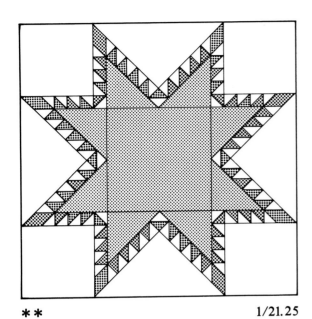

** ✱ ✱ **   1/21.25

COLOR: Instructions for this block are written for two colors of fabric — a light and a dark. You may use more colors if you wish.

CUTTING: Use templates 1-7 on pages 63-65. Cutting instructions assume that you will be using a bias-strip piecing to make the two-triangle feather units. Refer to page 56 for bias-strip piecing instructions.

Cut these pieces for one 21 1/4" Feathered Star block:

    Template #1: 28 bias-cut units
                  #1A: 8 light
                  #2: 36 bias-cut units
                  #2A: 8 light
                  #3: 4 dark, R 4 dark
                  #4: 4 light
                  #5: 4 light
                  #6: 8 dark
                  #7: 1 dark

FEATHERED STAR I

21 1/4" block

This is the center block for the Feathered Star with Pineapple Border. Instructions for the entire quilt begin on page 101.

VARIATION: For a Variable Star center, replace Template #7 with an 8" Variable Star block made from Templates #11-14 on page 65.

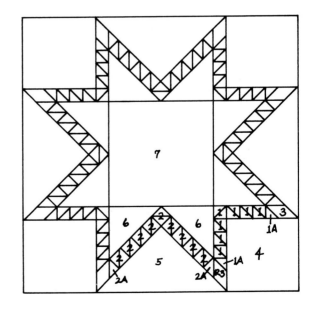

PIECING

1. Unit A, the star center, is a plain square cut with Template #7.

Unit A:
Center

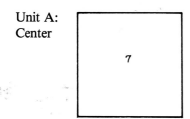

2. Make four B units. For each, piece the feather rows as shown using #2 bias-cut feather units and #2A triangles. Attach the feather rows to the #5 triangles with halfway seams. Add two #6 triangles.

Unit B:
Make 4

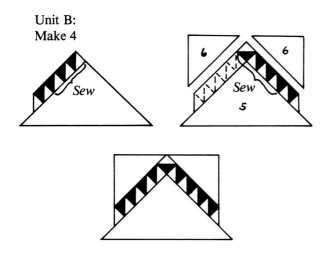

3. Make four C units. Matching center notches, sew the #1A triangles to the #3 parallelograms. Four of these units will be the reverse of the other four. Following the diagram, complete the feather rows with #1 bias-cut units. Sew the #1 feather rows to the #4 corner squares.

Make 4 each

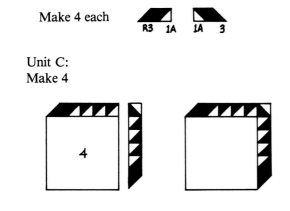

Unit C:
Make 4

4. Sew the A, B, and C units together in rows as shown. Sew the long seams to join the rows together. Sew the remaining portions of the halfway seams last.

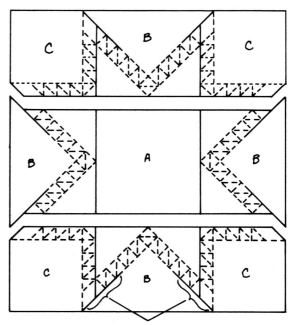

*Sew remaining portions
of these seams last.*

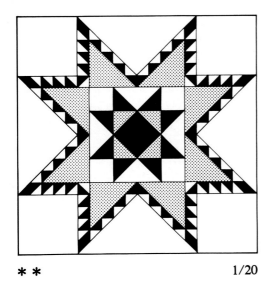

** ★ ★ **   1/20

COLOR: Instructions for this block are written for three colors — a light, a medium, and a dark. Use just two colors or add more if you wish.

CUTTING: Use Templates #1, 1A, 5, 6, and 8-14 on pages 63-65. Cutting instructions assume that you will be using bias-strip piecing to make the two-triangle sawtooth feather units. Refer to page 56 for bias-strip piecing instructions. Note that there are also dogtooth feathers in this pattern. They are cut and pieced in the conventional manner.

Cut these pieces for one 20" Feathered Variable Star block:

Template: #1: 28 bias cuts
           #1A: 40 light, 24 dark
           #5: 4 light
           #6: 8 medium
           #8: 4 light
           #9: 4 R 4 dark
           #10: 4 dark
           #11: 4 light
           #12: 4 light
           #13: 4 medium, 8 dark
           #14: 1 dark

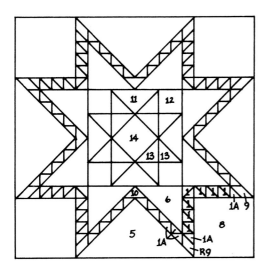

FEATHERED VARIABLE STAR

20" block

This design has both dogtooth and sawtooth feathers. The Variable Star center also could be used in the 20 1/4" Feathered Star on page 60.

VARIATION: For a plain center, use Template #7 on page 64 to replace the center 8" Variable Star in this design. Or use the 8" Rising Star Center shown on page 72.

PIECING

1. Unit A, the star center, is an 8" Variable Star block. Piece it according to the piecing sequence provided.

Unit A: Center
Make 1

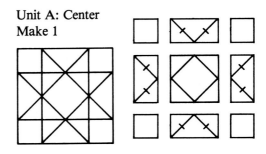

2. Make four B units. For each, make the dogtooth feather rows as shown, using triangles cut with Template #1A. Attach the feather rows to the #5 triangle, using halfway seams. Add triangle #10, then add the #6 triangles.

Unit B:
Make 4

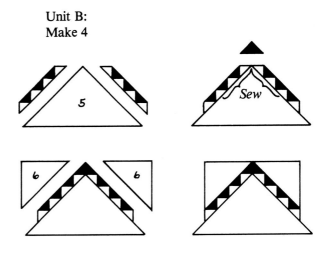

3. Make four C units. Matching center notches, sew the #1A triangles to the #9 parallelograms. Four of these units will be the reverse of the other four. Complete the feather rows with # bias-cut feather units. Sew the feather rows to the #8 corner squares.

Make 4 each

Unit C:
Make 4

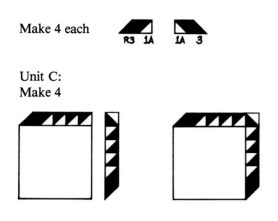

4. Join the A, B, and C units together in rows as shown. Sew the long seams to join the rows. Sew the remaining portions of the halfway seams last.

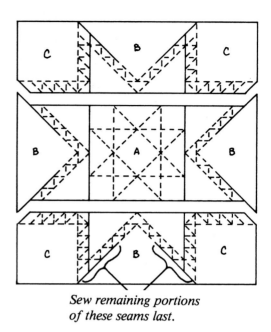

Sew remaining portions of these seams last.

TEMPLATES

straight grain

#6

1/4" seam allowance

#5

fold

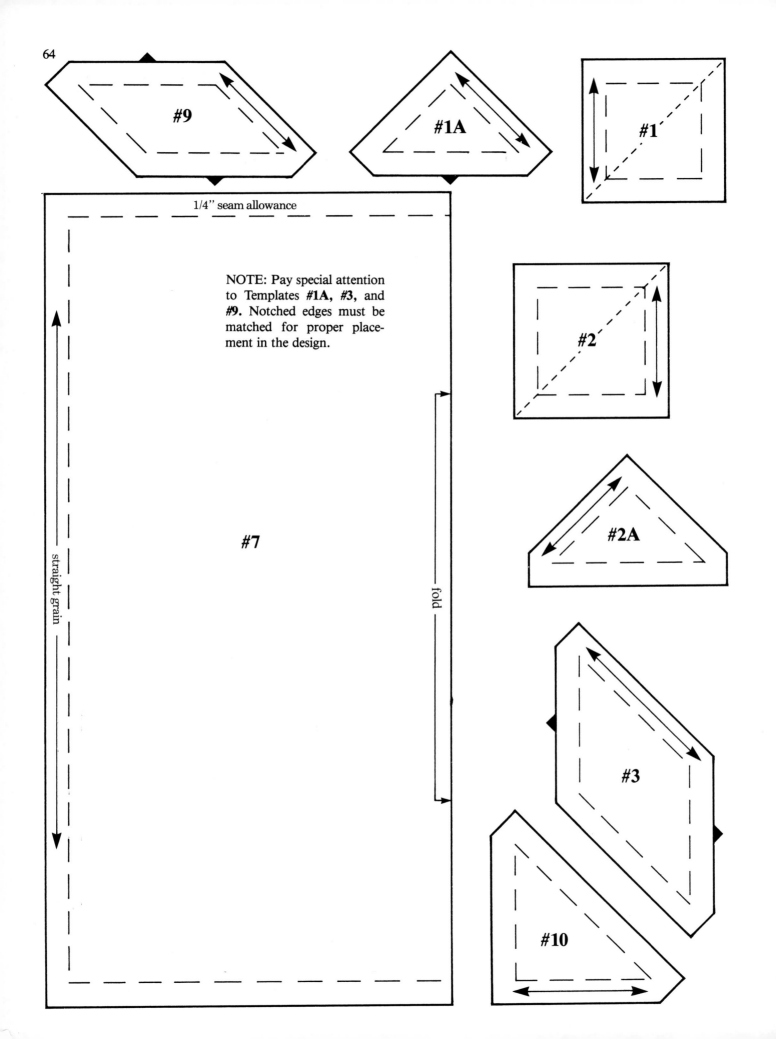

#9

#1A

#1

1/4" seam allowance

NOTE: Pay special attention to Templates **#1A, #3,** and **#9.** Notched edges must be matched for proper placement in the design.

#2

#7

straight grain

fold

#2A

#3

#10

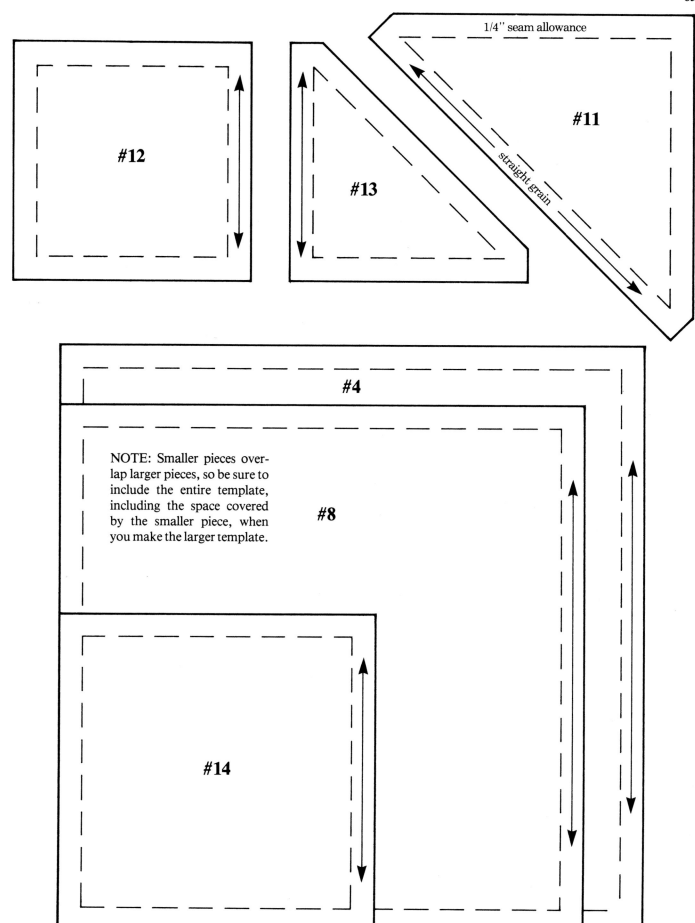

1/4" seam allowance

#11

straight grain

#12

#13

#4

#8

NOTE: Smaller pieces overlap larger pieces, so be sure to
include the entire template,
including the space covered
by the smaller piece, when
you make the larger template.

#14

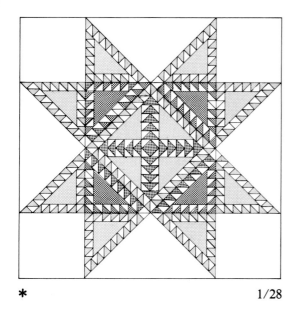

*   1/28

STAR SPANGLED BANNER

28" block

There are 629 pieces in this 28" version of the Star Spangled Banner. Bias-strip piecing described on page 56 reduces the actual number of pieces cut to 381 — a sizeable reduction in work that makes the block more feasible as a quilt pattern.

COLOR: Instructions here are written for a three-color design — light, medium, and dark fabric are used.

CUTTING: Use Templates #1-7 on pages 67-68. Cutting notations are given assuming that bias-strip piecing will be used for the feather units.

For one 28" Star Spangled Banner block, cut these pieces:
Template #1: 1 dark
        #2: 36 light, 16 medium, 8 dark
        #2A: 36 dark-and-light bias-cut units,
             72 medium-and-light bias cut units
        #3: 20 dark
        #4: 4 dark, 12 medium
        #5: 12 light, 8 medium, 4 dark
        #5A: 108 medium-and-light bias-cut units,
             32 dark-and-light bias-cut units
        #6: 4 light
        #7: 4 light

PIECING

1. Make one center Section A.

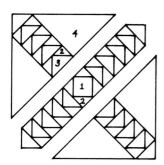

2. Border Section A with medium and light sawtooth sections made of bias-cut squares. Use Template #5A.

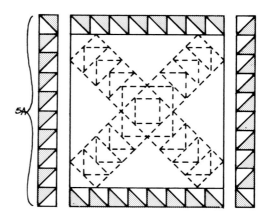

3. Piece four B sections of dark and light.

Section B. Make 4

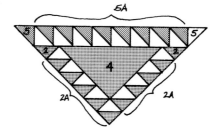

NOTE: Templates #2A and #5A are slightly different sizes. Take care not to mix them up.

4. Piece four C sections and four D sections. These sections form the eight points of the star, but notice they are mirror images. If they were exactly the same, every other tip of the star would be light instead of medium and would "disappear" into the light background fabric.

5. Join all sections with corner squares (#6) and side triangles (#7) as shown to complete star.

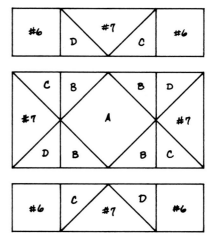

Make 4 Section C   Make 4 Section D

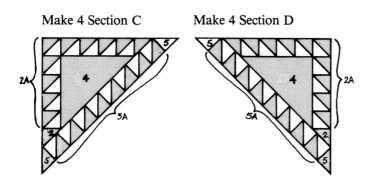

TEMPLATES

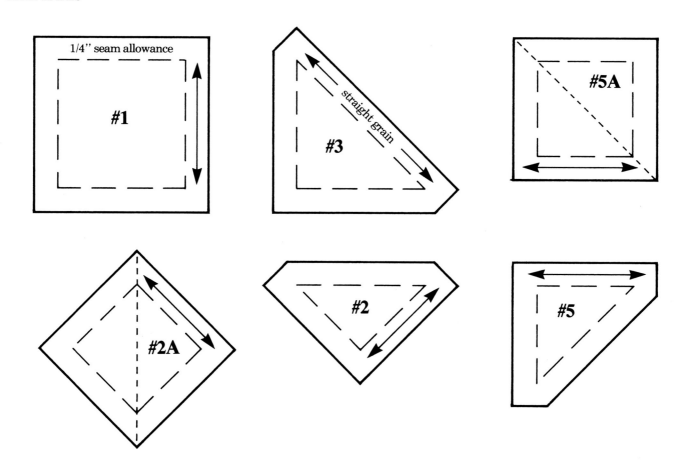

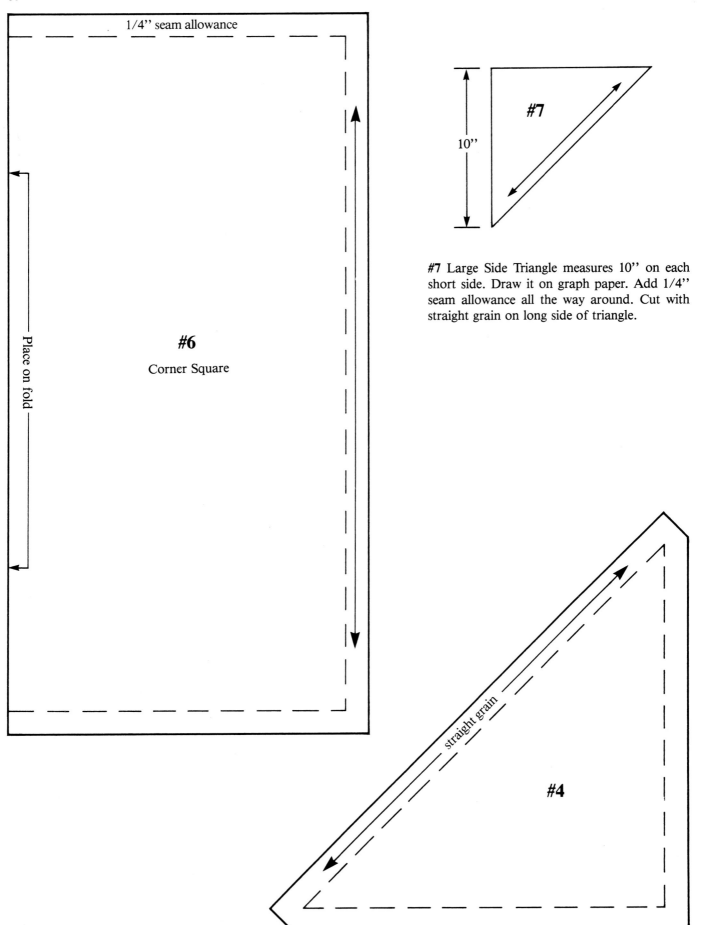

1/4'' seam allowance

#6

Corner Square

Place on fold

#7 Large Side Triangle measures 10'' on each short side. Draw it on graph paper. Add 1/4'' seam allowance all the way around. Cut with straight grain on long side of triangle.

#7

10''

straight grain

#4

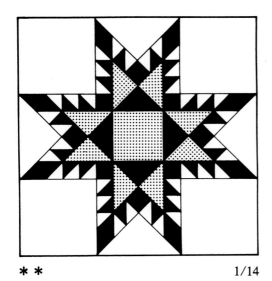

**   1/14

FEATHER EDGE STAR

14" block

This star block and the next nine blocks share many of the same templates. They are identified by bold-faced capital letters and begin on page 81.

COLOR: Instructions for this block are written for three colors — a light, a medium, and a dark. Use just two colors or add more if you like.

CUTTING: Use Templates **A, A1, B, B1, C, D, E, F,** and **G** on pages 81-85. Cutting instructions assume that you will be using bias-strip piecing to make the two-triangle feather units. Refer to page 56 for bias-strip piecing instructions.

Cut these pieces for one 14" Feather Edge Star block:
Template **A:** 16 bias-cut units, 4 dark squares
       A1: 8 light
       B: 8 bias-cut units, 4 dark squares
       B1: 8 light
       C: 4 dark, R 4 dark
       D: 8 medium, 4 dark
       E: 4 light
       F: 4 light
       G: 1 medium

PIECING

1. Unit A, the star center, is pieced as pictured, using square **G** and four **D** triangles.

Unit A: Make 1

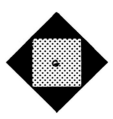

2. Make four B units. Matching double center notches, sew the **B1** triangles to the **C** parallelograms. Four of these units will be the reverse of the other four. Complete the rows of feathers as shown, using **B** bias-cut feather units and **B** squares. Sew the feather rows to the **E** triangles as shown.

Make 4 each

Unit B: Make 4

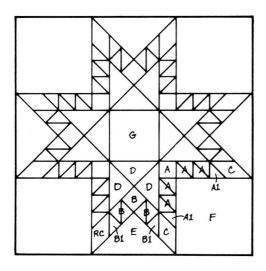

3. Make four C units. Make the feather rows as shown, using **A** bias-cut feather units and squares and **A1** triangles. Attach feather rows to the **F** corner square with halfway seams. Add **D** triangles.

Unit C: Make 4

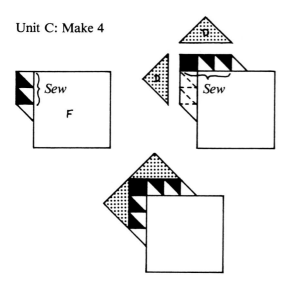

4. Sew the A, B, and C units together in diagonal rows as shown. Sew the long seams to join the rows. Sew the remaining portions of the halfway seams last.

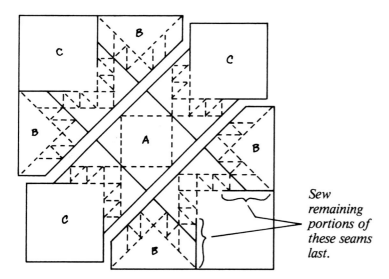

Sew remaining portions of these seams last.

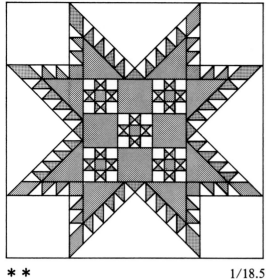

**   1/18.5

COLOR: Instructions for this block are written for two colors, a light and a dark. Choose more colors if you like.

CUTTING: Use templates **A, A1, B, B1, C, F, K, X, Y, Z,** and **AA** on pages 81-85. Cutting instructions are given, assuming bias-strip piecing will be used for the half-square triangle feather units. Also use bias-strip piecing to piece the quarter-square triangles in the small Variable Stars using Template **Z.** See page 56 for bias-strip piecing instructions.

Cut these pieces for one 18 1/2" California Star Block:
Template **A:** 16 bias-cut units, 4 dark squares
> **A1:** 8 light
> **B:** 32 bias-cut units
> **B1:** 8 light, 4 dark
> **C:** 4 dark, R 4 dark
> **K:** 8 dark
> **F:** 4 light
> **X:** 4 light
> **Y:** 20 light, 5 dark
> **Z:** 40 bias-cut quarter-square units
> **AA:** 4 dark

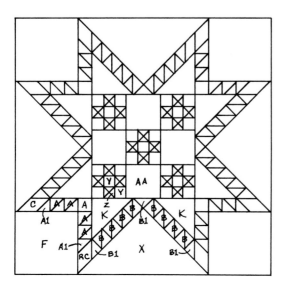

CALIFORNIA STAR

18 1/2" block

There are several versions of Feathered Stars that are called California Star. All are based on a grid star and have the large center square divided into a nine-patch. Most California Stars also display five tiny Variable Stars in the nine-patch squares. This pattern is like the example pictured on page 26. Another version is pictured on page 39.

PIECING

1. Unit A, the star center, is a nine-patch made of five small Variable Star blocks and four plain squares. Piece the center as pictured, using templates **Z, Y,** and **AA.**

Unit A: Center
Make 20

Make 5 small
Variable Star blocks

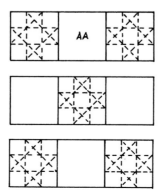

2. Make four B units. Make the feather rows as shown, using **B** bias-cut feather units and **B1** triangles. Attach the feather rows to the **X** side triangle with halfway seams. Add **K** triangles.

Unit B: Make 4

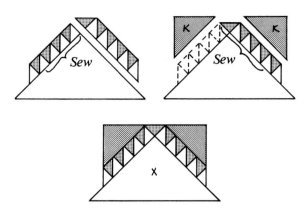

3. Make four C units. Matching center notches, sew the **A1** triangles to the **C** parallelograms. Four of these units will be the reverse of the other four. Complete the feather rows as shown, using **A** bias-cut units and **A** squares. Sew the feather rows to the **F** corner squares as shown.

Make 4 each

Unit C: Make 4

4. Sew the A, B, and C units together in rows as shown. Sew the rows together. Sew the remaining portions of the halfway seams last.

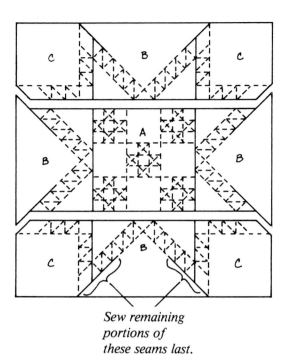

Sew remaining portions of these seams last.

Color variation

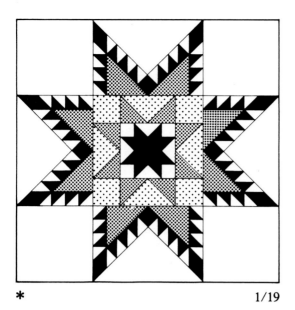

*   1/19

RISING STAR

19" block

It takes relatively few of these large Feathered Star blocks to make a quilt.

COLOR: Instructions for this block are written for four fabrics — a light background fabric, a slightly darker light print (medium light), a medium, and a dark.

CUTTING: Use templates **A, A1, B, B1, C, K, L, M, T, U, V,** and **W** on pages 81-85. Cutting instructions assume that you will be using bias-strip piecing to make the two-triangle feather units. Refer to page 56 for bias-strip piecing instructions.

Cut these pieces for one 19" Rising Star block:
Template **A:** 24 bias-cut units, 4 light squares
    A1: 8 light, 8 dark
    B: 24 bias-cut units, 4 dark squares
    B1: 8 light
    C: 4 dark, R 4 dark
    K: 8 medium
    L: 4 light
    M: 4 light
    T: 4 light
    U: 8 medium
    V: 4 medium light
    W: 4 medium light

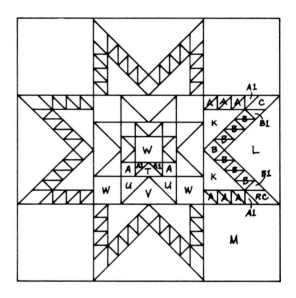

PIECING

1. Unit A, the center, is an 8" Rising Star block and is pieced according to the diagram shown.

Unit A: Make 1

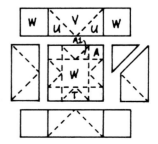

2. Make four B units. Matching the double center notches, sew the **B1** triangles to the **C** parallelograms. Four of these units will be the reverse of the other four. Complete the inner rows of feathers as shown, using **B** bias-cut feather units and **B** dark squares. Sew the **B** feather rows to the **L** triangle as shown. Using **A** bias-cut feather units and **A1** triangles, make the outer feather rows. Four of these units will be the reverse of the other four. Attach the **A** feather rows to the **K** triangles as shown. Add to previous piecing to complete Unit B.

Make 4 each

Unit B: Make 4

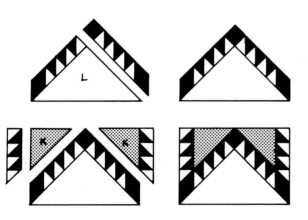

3. The four C units are unpieced squares cut with Template **M.**

Unit C: Cut 4

4. Sew the A, B, and C units together in rows as shown, then sew the long seams to join the rows.

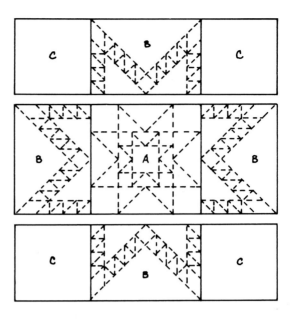

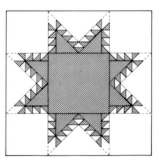

Phoenix Star

Phoenix Star II

VARIATIONS: Two block variations are shown here. In both, a plain center (Template **N**) has been substituted for the 8'' Rising Star center block. Further design changes have been made by changing the direction and coloring of the feathers.

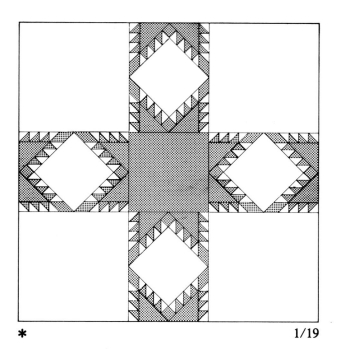

*   1/19

TOUCHING STARS

Bar quilt with 19" stars

Touching Stars is not a Feathered Star block design, but rather a bar-quilt design. Bar quilts are discussed on page 28. This is an old-fashioned looking pattern and looks great in just two colors with fancy quilting in the large background pieces.

COLOR: Instructions for this design are written for two colors.

CUTTING: Use templates **A, A1, B, B1, C, J, K, Mx4,** and **N** on pages 81-84. Cutting instructions assume that bias-strip piecing will be used to make the two-triangle feather units. Refer to page 56 for bias-strip piecing instructions.

Cut these pieces for one B unit of the Touching Stars design:
Template **A:** 12 bias-cut units

    A1: 4 light

    B: 12 bias-cut units, 2 dark squares

    B1: 4 light

    C: 2 dark, R 2 dark

    J: 1 light

    K: 4 dark

PIECING

1. Unit A, the star center, is a single large, unpieced square cut with Template **N**.

2. Four B units are needed to make a complete star, but each B unit contains points of two stars. To make one B unit, first sew the **B1** triangles to the **C** parallelograms matching double notched edges. Make four — two will be the reverse of the other two. Complete the inner feather rows, using **B** feather units and **B** squares. Sew the **B** feather rows to square **J**. Using **A** feather units and **A1** triangles, make the outer feather rows. Two of these units will be the reverse of the other two. Attach the **A** feather rows to the **K** triangles as shown. Add to previous piecing to complete unit B.

3. Unit C, which forms the corners of four stars at once, is cut with Template **Mx4**.

Make 2 each

                                RC B1   B1 C

Unit B:

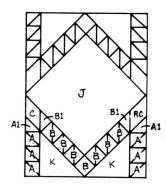

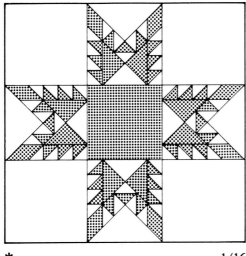

*   1/16

JOINING STAR

16" and 12" blocks

The Joining Star pattern is offered in two sizes and is readily adaptable to bar-quilt construction. A Joining Stars bar quilt by Beverly Bynum is shown on page 28. Instructions for the quilt are on page 105.

COLOR: Instructions are given for two colors. Use more fabrics if you wish.

CUTTING: To make a 16" block, use Templates **A, A1, B, B1, C, D, E, M,** and **O** on pages 81-85. Templates for the 12" version of the block begin on page 85 and are designated by lowercase bold face letters. Cutting instructions are given, assuming bias-strip piecing will be used to make the half-square triangle feather units. (See page 56 for bias-strip piecing.)

Cut these pieces for one 16" Joining Star block (12" block templates are in parentheses):
Template **A (a):** 24 bias-cut units
    A1 (a1): 8 light
    B (b): 12 bias-cut units
    B1 (b1): 8 light
    C (c): 4 dark, R 4 dark
    D (d): 8 dark, 4 light
    E (e): 4 light
    M (m): 4 light
    O (o): 1 dark

PIECING

1. Unit A is a plain square cut with Template **O**.

    Unit A: Cut 1

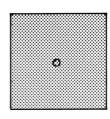

2. Make four B units. Matching double center notches, sew the **B1** triangles to the **C** parallelograms. Four of these units will be the reverse of the other four. Complete the feather rows as shown, using **B** feather units. Sew the **B** feather rows to triangle **E**. Make rows using **A** feather units and **A1** triangles as shown. Sew the **A** feather rows to the **D** triangles and complete the B units.

Make 4 each

Unit B: Make 4

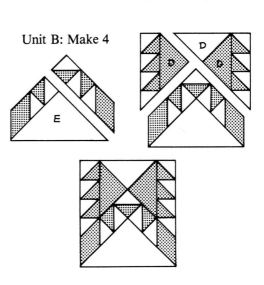

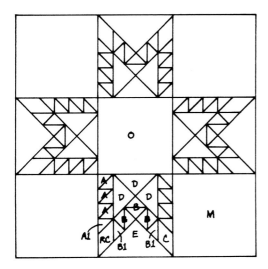

3. Make four C units. The four corners are plain squares cut with Template **M.**

Unit C: Cut 4

4. Sew the completed A, B, and C units together in rows as shown. Sew the rows together to complete the block.

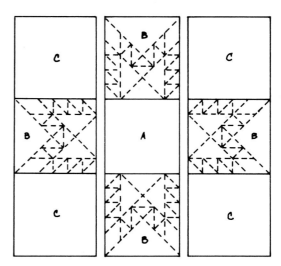

FEATHER STARS

There are four Feather Star patterns offered here. Each has a different center. All four blocks are in the Feathered Star Sampler pictured on page 12 and are offered in both 16'' and 12'' sizes. Because these blocks are identical except for the centers, piecing instructions are given only once.

COLOR: Instructions for these blocks are written for two colors, a light and a dark. Use more colors if you like.

CUTTING: Templates for the 16'' Feather Stars begin on page 81 and are designated by bold face capital letters. Templates for the 12'' blocks begin on page 85 and are designated by bold-faced lowercase letters. Cutting instructions are given, assuming bias-strip piecing will be used for the half-square triangle feather units (see page 56).

FEATHER STAR

16'' and 12'' blocks

Cut these pieces for one 16'' Feather Star block (12'' block templates are in parentheses):

Template **A (a):** 24 bias-cut units
    A1 (a1): 8 light, 4 dark
    B (b): 8 bias-cut units, 4 dark squares
    B1 (b1): 8 light
    C (c): 4 dark, R 4 dark
    D (d): 8 dark
    E (e): 4 light
    J (j): 1 dark
    M (m): 4 light

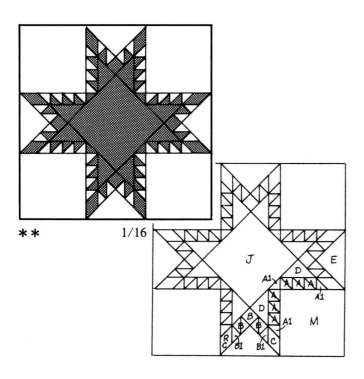

**   1/16

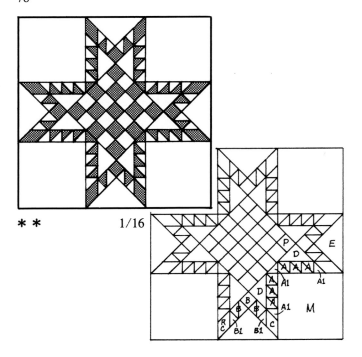

** 1/16

FEATHER STAR WITH TWENTY-FIVE-PATCH CENTER

16" and 12" blocks

Cut these pieces for one 16" Feather Star With Twenty-Five-Patch Center block (12" block templates are in parentheses):

Template **A (a):** 24 bias-cut units
  A1 (a1): 8 light, 4 dark
  B (b): 8 bias-cut units, 4 dark squares
  B1 (b1): 8 light
  C (c): 4 dark, R 4 dark
  D (d): 8 light
  E (e): 4 light
  M (m): 4 light
  P (p): 12 light, 14 dark

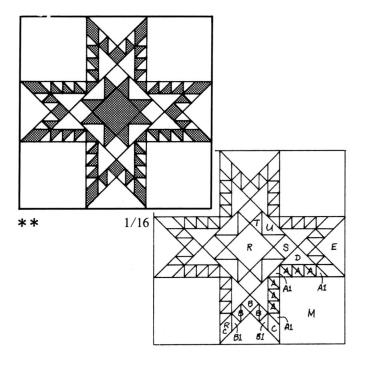

** 1/16

FEATHER STAR WITH MORNING STAR CENTER

16" and 12" blocks

Cut these pieces for one 16" Feather Star With Morning Star Center block (12" block templates are in parentheses):

Template **A (a):** 24 bias-cut units
  A1 (a1): 8 light, 4 dark
  B (b): 8 bias-cut units, 4 dark squares
  B1 (b1): 8 light
  C (c): 4 dark, R 4 dark
  D (d): 8 light
  E (e): 4 light
  M (m): 4 light
  R (r): 1 dark
  S (s): 4 light
  T (t): 8 dark
  U (u): 4 light

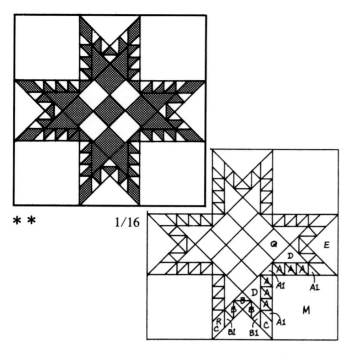

** 1/16

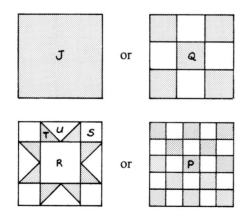

FEATHER STAR WITH NINE-PATCH CENTER

16" and 12" blocks

Cut these pieces for one 16" Feather Star With Nine-Patch Center block (12" block templates are in parentheses):

Template **A (a):** 24 bias-cut units
    A1 (a1): 8 light, 4 dark
    B (b): 12 bias-cut units
    B1 (b1): 8 light
    C (c): 4 dark, R 4 dark
    D (d): 8 dark
    E (e): 4 light
    M (m): 4 light
    Q (q): 5 dark, 4 light

3. Make four C units. Make feather rows, using **A** feather units and **A1** triangles. Sew **A** feather rows to square **M** with halfway seams. Add **D** triangles as shown.

Unit C: Make 4

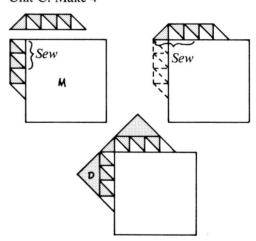

PIECING

1. Unit A is the center of each Feather Star. Choose one center option and piece as shown in the diagrams.

Unit A: Center (Plain or Pieced)

Make 1

4. Sew the completed A, B, and C units together in diagonal rows as shown. Sew long seams joining the rows. Complete halfway seams last.

2. Make four B units. Matching double center notches, sew **B1** triangles to **C** parallelograms. Four of these units will be the reverse of the other four. Complete the feather rows, using **B** feather units and squares. Sew completed **B** feather rows to triangle **E**.

Make 4 each

RC B1   B1 C

Unit B: Make 4

Sew remaining portions of these seams last.

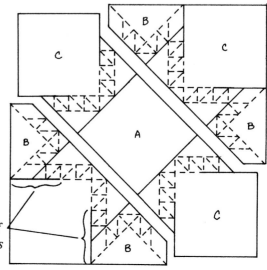

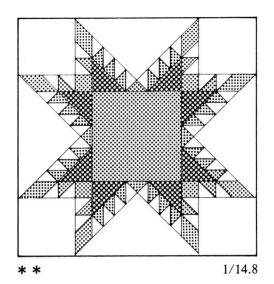

**   1/14.8

STAR OF CHAMBLIE

14.8'' block

Instructions for a quilt using this block are on page 104.

VARIATION: To change the center of this block, substitute the Nine-Patch Center on page 79, the Twenty-five-Patch Center on page 78, or the Morning Star Center on page 78 for Template **J.**

COLOR: Instructions for this block are written for two colors, with the idea that dark means scraps of many dark fabrics and light means many light fabrics.

CUTTING: Use templates **A, A1, B, B1, C, D, H, I,** and **J** on pages 81-85. Cutting instructions assume that bias-strip piecing will be used to make the two-triangle feather units. Refer to page 56 for bias-strip piecing instructions.

Cut these pieces for one 14.8'' Star of Chamblie block:
Template **A**: 24 bias-cut units
      A1: 8 light, 4 dark
      B: 8 bias-cut units, 4 dark squares
      B1: 8 light
      C: 4 dark, R 4 dark
      D: 8 dark
      H: 4 light
      I: 4 light
      J: 1 dark

PIECING

1. Unit A, the star center, is a plain square cut with Template J.

Unit A: Cut 1

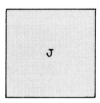

2. Make four B units. Make the feather rows as shown, using **A** bias-cut units and **A1** triangles. Attach the feather rows to the large **I** side triangle with halfway seams (see page 58). Add two **D** triangles.

Unit B: Make 4

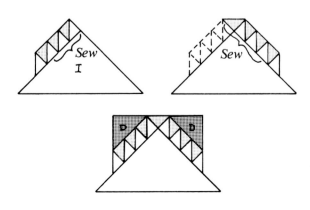

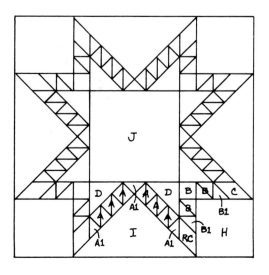

3. Make four C units. Matching double center notches, sew the **B1** triangles to the **C** parallelograms. Four of these units will be the reverse of the other four. Complete the feather rows as shown, using **B** bias-cut units and **B** squares. Sew the feather rows to the **H** corner square as shown.

Make 4 each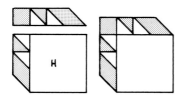

RC B1   B1 C

Unit C: Make 4

4. Sew the A, B, and C units together in rows as shown. Sew the remaining portions of the halfway seams last.

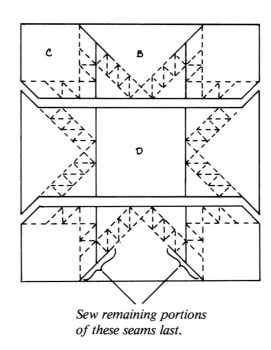

Sew remaining portions of these seams last.

TEMPLATES

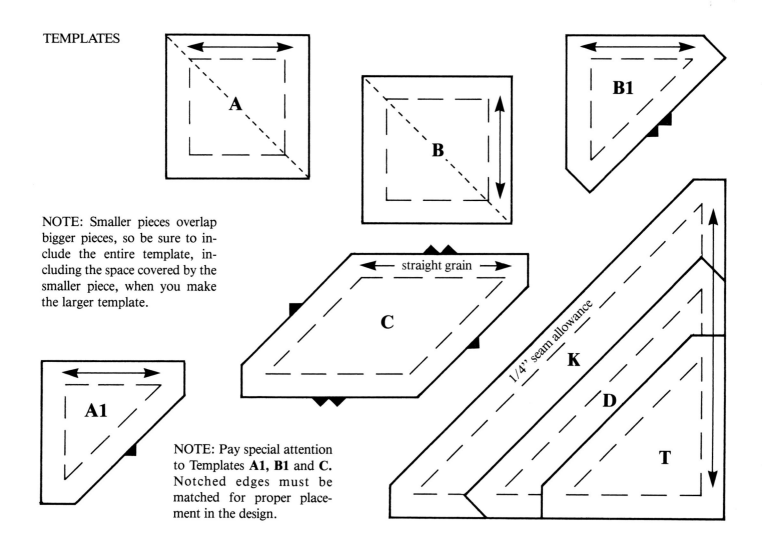

NOTE: Smaller pieces overlap bigger pieces, so be sure to include the entire template, including the space covered by the smaller piece, when you make the larger template.

NOTE: Pay special attention to Templates **A1, B1** and **C**. Notched edges must be matched for proper placement in the design.

NOTE: Smaller pieces overlap bigger pieces, so be sure to include the entire template, including the space covered by the smaller piece, when you make the larger template.

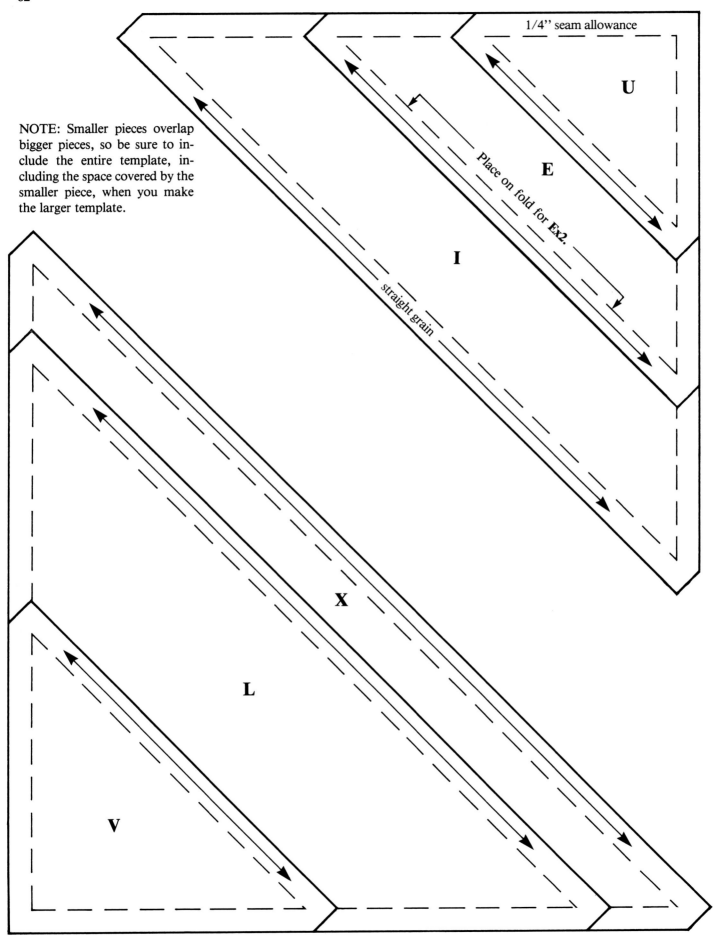

1/4'' seam allowance

U

E

I

Place on fold for Ex2.

straight grain

X

L

V

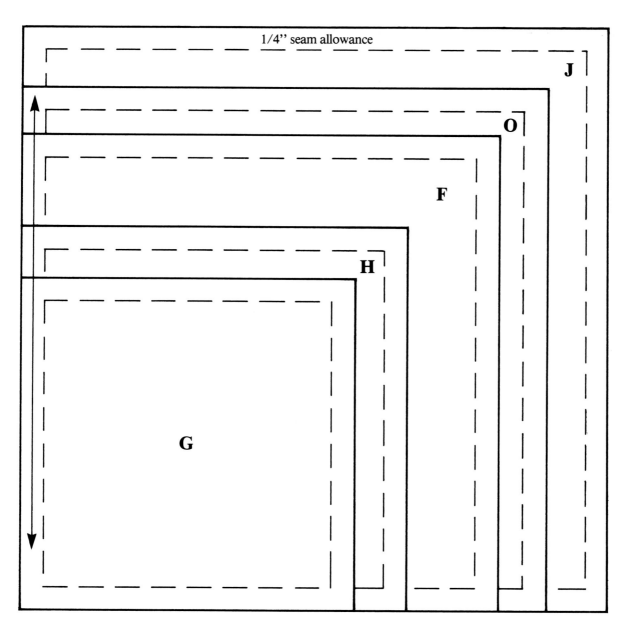

1/4'' seam allowance

J

O

F

H

G

NOTE: Smaller pieces overlap bigger pieces, so be sure to include the entire template, including the space covered by the smaller piece, when you make the larger template.

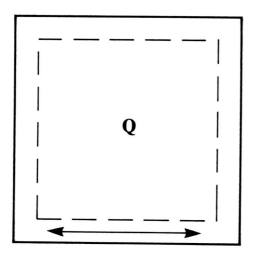

Q

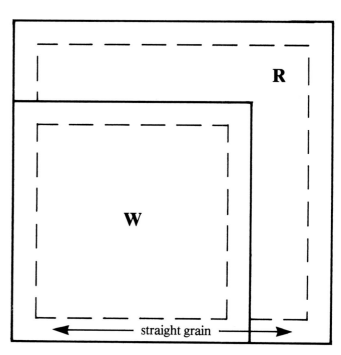

R

W

straight grain

84

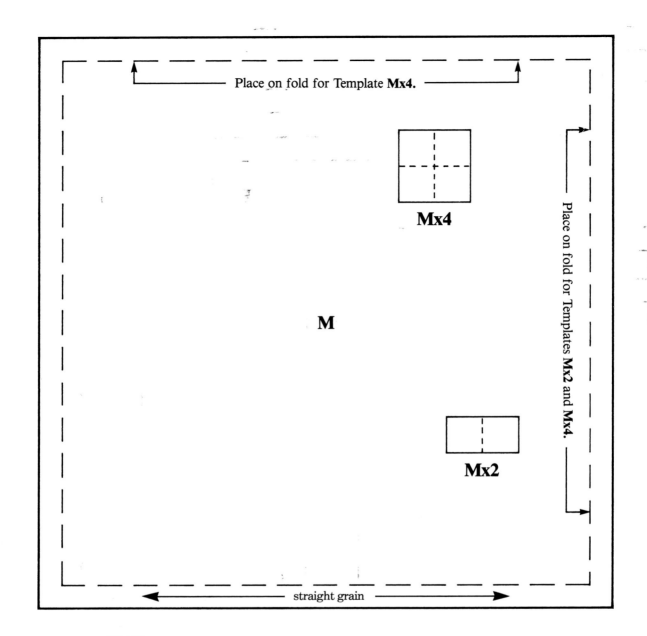

Place on fold for Template **Mx4.**

Mx4

M

Place on fold for Templates **Mx2** and **Mx4.**

Mx2

straight grain

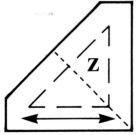

Z

NOTE: Smaller pieces overlap bigger pieces, so be sure to include the entire template, including the space covered by the smaller piece, when you make the larger template.

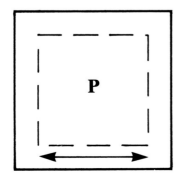

P

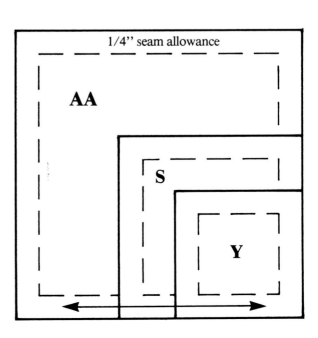

1/4'' seam allowance

AA

S

Y

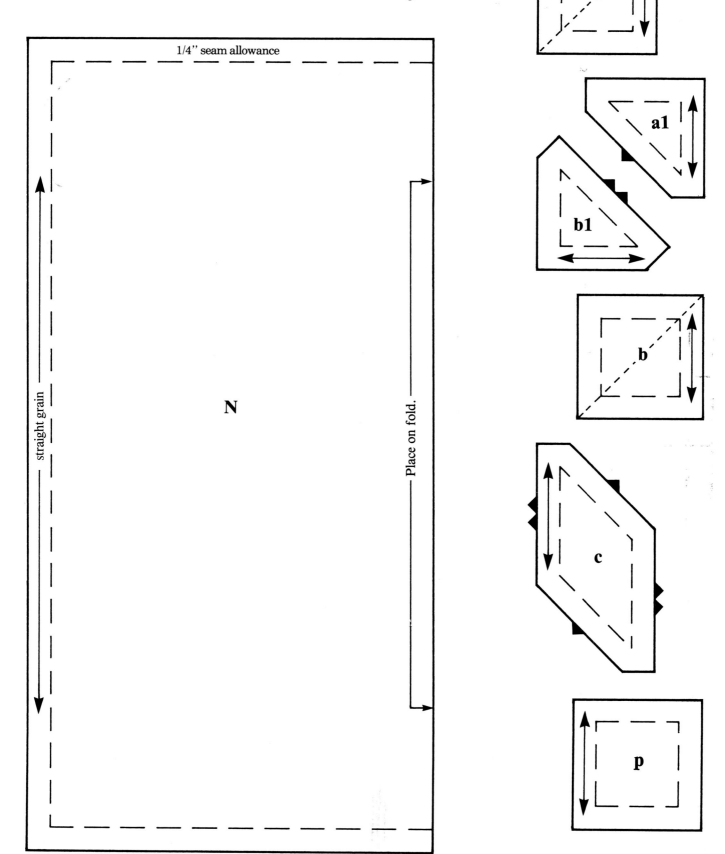

NOTE: Pay special attention to Templates **a1, b1** and **c.** Notched edges must be matched for proper placement in the design.

1/4" seam allowance

straight grain

N

Place on fold.

a

a1

b1

b

c

p

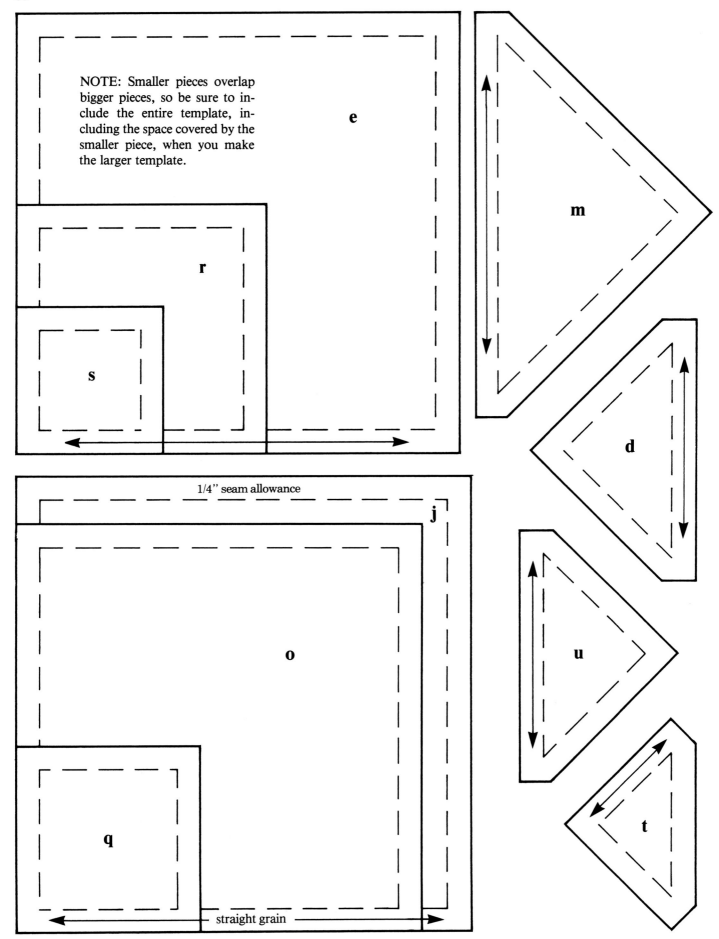

NOTE: Smaller pieces overlap bigger pieces, so be sure to include the entire template, including the space covered by the smaller piece, when you make the larger template.

e

r

s

m

d

u

t

1/4" seam allowance

j

o

q

straight grain

*   1.5/12

SAWTOOTH STAR

12" block

The Sawtooth Star is very simple as Feathered Stars go: it has sawtooth edges on only one side of the star points.

COLOR: Instructions for this block are written for three colors — a light, a medium, and a dark tone.

CUTTING: Use Templates #1-5 on the next page. Cutting notations are given, assuming that bias-strip piecing will be used for the half-square triangle feather units.

For one 12" Sawtooth Star block, cut these pieces:
Template #1: 16 bias-cut units, 4 light squares
    #1A: 8 dark
    #2: 4 light, 8 medium
    #3: 4 light
    #4: 4 light, 4 medium
    #5: 1 dark

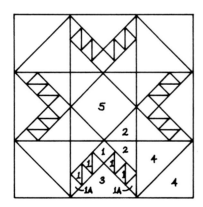

PIECING

1. Unit A, the star center, is pieced as shown, using a #5 square and four light #2 triangles.

Unit A: Make 1

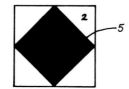

2. Make four B units. Make the feather rows as shown, using #1 bias-cut feather units, #1 squares, and #1A triangles. Sew feather rows to #3 triangles. Add #2 triangles.

Unit B: Make 4

3. Make four C units. Piece the corner units using #4 medium and light triangles.

Unit C: Make 4

4. Join the A, B, and C units together in rows as shown. Sew the long seams to join the rows.

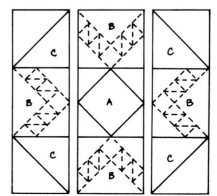

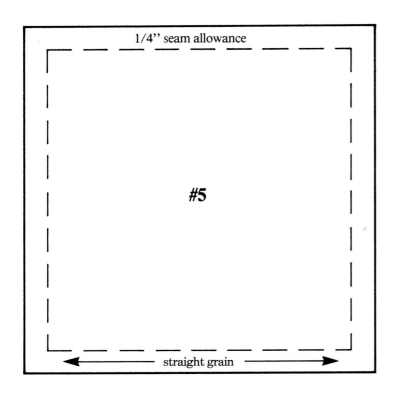

1/4'' seam allowance

#5

straight grain

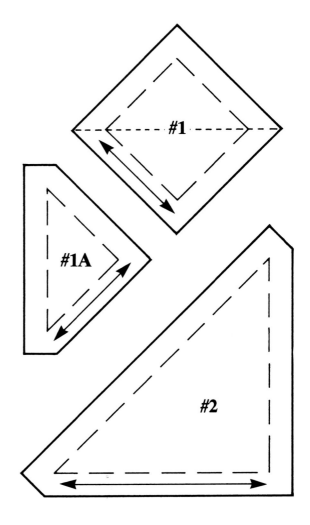

#1

#1A

#2

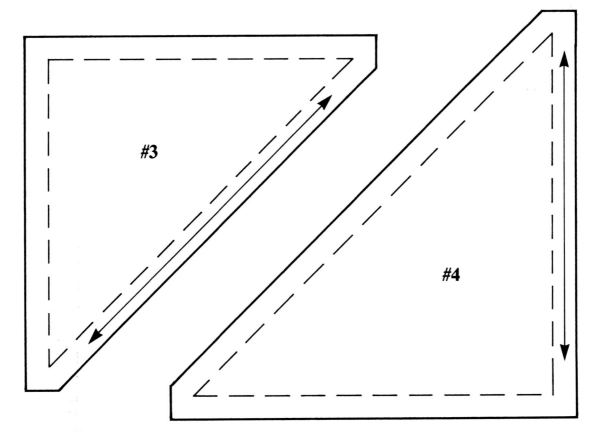

#3

#4

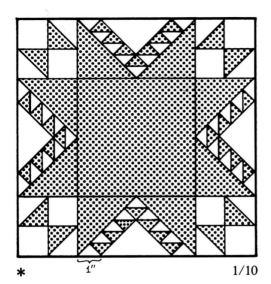

*   ⌐1"⌐   1/10

TWINKLING STAR

10" block

This pattern and the wall quilt pictured on page 43 (instructions are on page 107) were inspired by a quilt from the collection of the Oregon Historical Society.

COLOR: Instructions for this block are written for a two-color design. Use more fabrics if you wish.

CUTTING: Use Templates #1-5 on the next page. Cutting notations are given, assuming that bias-strip piecing will be used for the feather units

For one 10" Twinkling Star block, cut these pieces:
Template #1: 28 bias-cut units
    #1A: 8 light
    #2: 4 light
    #3: 8 dark
    #4: 8 bias-cut units, 8 light squares
    #5: 1 dark

2. Make four B units. Make feather rows as shown, using #1 bias-cut feather units and #1A triangles. Sew to #2 triangle. Add #3 triangles.

Unit B:
Make 4

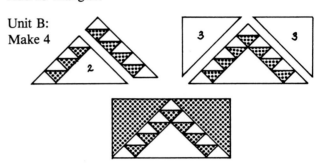

3. Make four C units. Use Template #4 to make both squares and bias-cut half-square triangles. Piece as shown.

Unit C: Make 4

4. Sew units A, B, and C in rows as shown. Sew the long seams to join the rows.

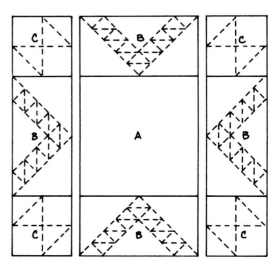

PIECING

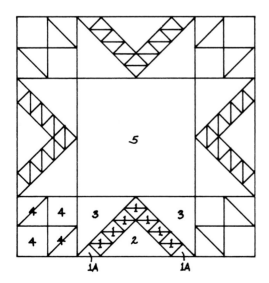

1. Unit A, the star center, is a large unpieced square cut with Template #5.

Unit A: Cut 1

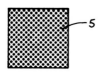

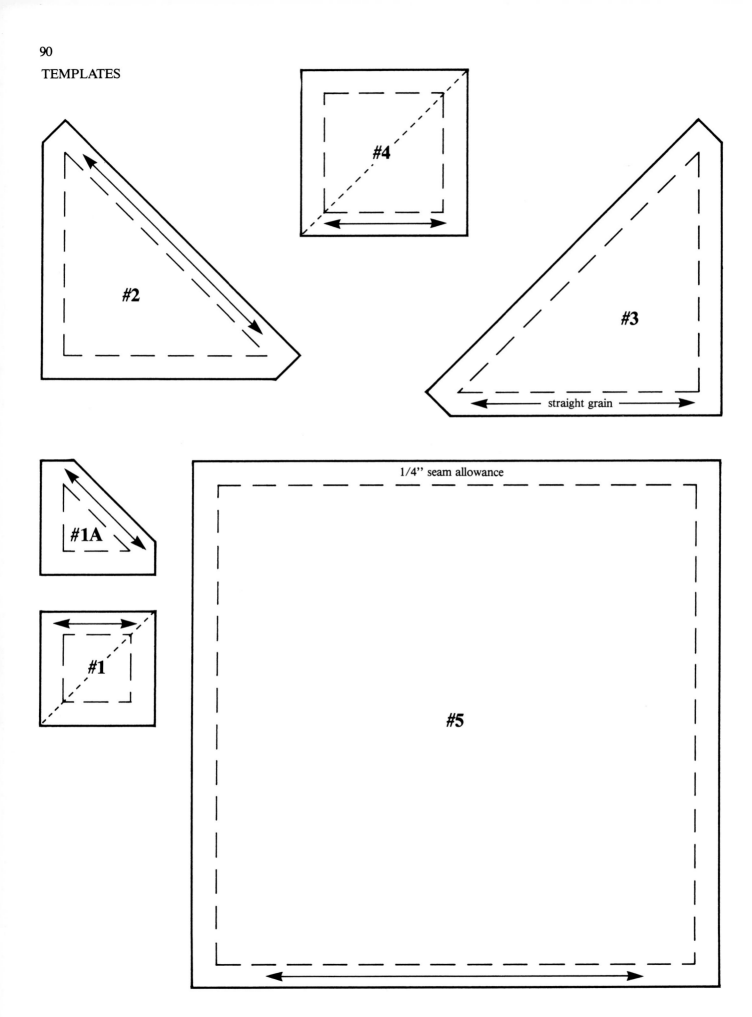

#4

#2

#3

straight grain

#1A

1/4'' seam allowance

#1

#5

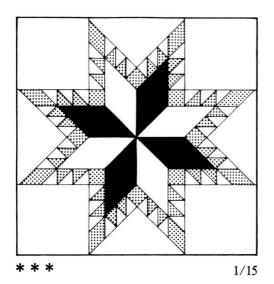

* * *   1/15

COLOR: Instructions are written for three colors — a light, a medium, and a dark tone.

CUTTING: Templates for the 15" block are on pages 96-99 and are designated by bold face capital letters. Templates for the 12" block begin on page 99 and are designated by bold face lowercase letters. For the 15" block use templates **A**, **A1**, **B**, **E**, **F**, and **H**. For the 12" block, use templates **a**, **a1**, **b**, **e**, **f**, and **h**. Cutting instructions are given, assuming bias-strip piecing will be used for making the feather units.

For one 15" Feathered Le Moyne Star, cut these pieces (12" block templates are in parentheses):

Template **A (a):** 32 bias-cut units, 8 dark squares

    A1 (a1): 16 light
    B (b): 8 dark
    E (e): 4 light
    F (f): 4 light
    H (h): 4 light, 4 medium

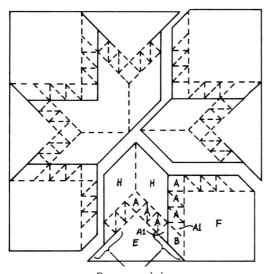

Sew remaining portions of these seams last.

FEATHERED LE MOYNE STAR

15" and 12" blocks

This design is offered in two sizes and shares some templates with the next pattern, the Radiant Star or Chestnut Burr.

PIECING

1. Make four A units. First, piece feather rows as shown, using **A** bias-cut feather units, **A** squares, and **A1** triangles. Attach the feather rows to the **E** triangles, using halfway seams. Sew **H** diamonds to previous piecing (this requires set-in seams).

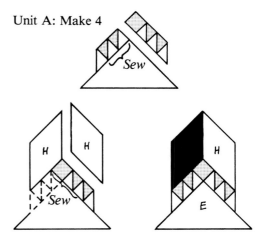

Unit A: Make 4

2. Make four B units. Sew **A1** triangles to **B** diamonds. Four of these units will be the reverse of the other four. Complete the feather rows, using **A** bias-cut feather units and **A** squares. Sew feather rows as shown to the **F** corner squares.

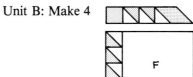

Make 4 each

Unit B: Make 4

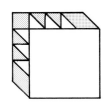

3. Join the A and B units as shown, using set-in seams. Complete halfway seams last.

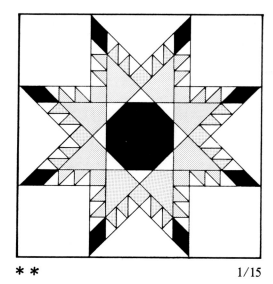

**   1/15

RADIANT STAR

15" and 12" blocks

Also known as a Chestnut Burr, or a Star of Bethlehem, this is one of the loveliest of the Feathered Star designs. It is offered here in two sizes.

COLOR: Instructions are given for three colors — a light, a medium, and a dark fabric.

CUTTING: Templates for the 15" block are on pages 96-99 and are designated by bold face capital letters. Templates for the 12" block begin on page 99 and are designated by bold face lowercase letters. For the 15" block use templates **A, A1, B, C, D, E, F,** and **G.** For the 12" block, use templates **a, a1, b, c, d, e, f,** and **g.** Cutting instructions are given, assuming bias-strip piecing will be used for making the feather units.

For one 15" Radiant Star, cut these pieces (12" block templates are in parentheses):
Template **A (a):** 32 bias-cut units, 8 medium squares
> **A1 (a1):** 16 light
> **B (b):** 8 dark
> **C (c):** 8 medium
> **D (d):** 8 light
> **E (e):** 4 light
> **F (f):** 4 light
> **G (g):** 1 dark

PIECING

1. Unit A, the star center, is octagon **G** with 4 **D** triangles sewn on to make it a square.

Unit A: Center — Make 1

2. Make four B units. Piece the feather rows as shown, using **A** bias-cut feather units, **A** squares, and **A1** triangles. Attach the feather rows to the **E** triangles using halfway seams. Add the **C** kite shapes and **D** triangles as shown.

Unit B: Make 4

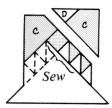

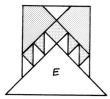

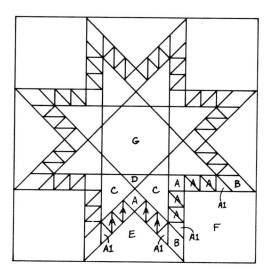

3. Make four C units. Sew **A1** triangles to **B** diamonds. Four of these units will be the reverse of the other four. Complete the feather rows, using **A** bias-cut feather units and **A** squares. Sew feather rows as shown to **F** corner squares.

Make 4 each

Unit C: Make 4

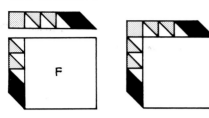

4. Sew the A, B, and C units together in rows as shown. Join the rows by sewing the long seams. Finish halfway seams last.

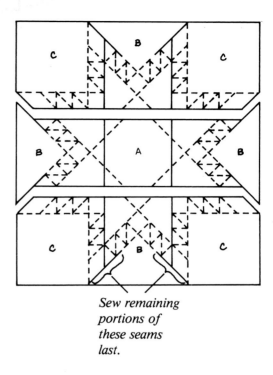

Sew remaining portions of these seams last.

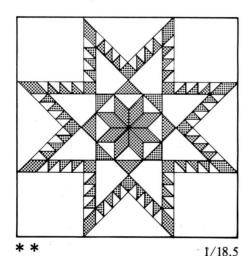

**   1/18.5

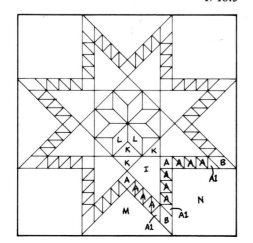

FEATHERED STAR WITH LE MOYNE STAR CENTER

18 1/2" block

These large Feathered Star blocks and the next one are the same size. They share templates with each other and with the two previous patterns. (Templates begin on page 99.) Feathered Star II and Feathered Star With Le Moyne Star Center are identical except for their centers, so piecing instructions are given for both blocks on page 94.

COLOR: Instructions are given for two colors, a light and a dark. Use more fabrics if you wish.

CUTTING: Templates begin on page 96. For Feathered Star With Le Moyne Star Center use **A, A1, B, I, K, L, M,** and **N.** Instructions are given assuming bias-strip piecing will be used for the feather units.

For one 18 1/2" Feathered Star with Le Moyne Star Center, cut these pieces:

Template **A**: 48 bias-cut units, 8 dark squares
    A1: 16 light
    B: 8 dark
    I: 8 light
    K: 8 light, 8 dark
    L: 8 dark
    M: 4 light
    N: 4 light

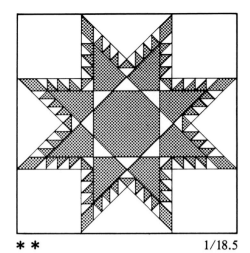

**   1/18.5

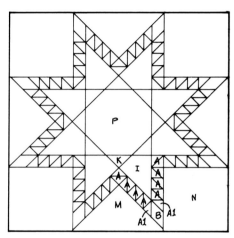

PIECING

1. Unit A, the star center, can be either a plain octagon or a small Le Moyne Star. Choose one center and piece as shown.

Unit A: Center

Make 1

or

2. Make four B units. Make feather rows as shown, using **A** bias-cut units, **A1** triangles, and **A** squares if called for. Attach feather rows to **M** triangles with halfway seams. Add **I** kite shapes and **K** triangles as shown.

Unit B: Make 4

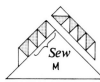
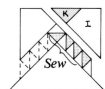
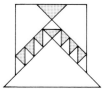

FEATHERED STAR II

18 1/2'' block

COLOR: Instructions are given for two colors, a light and a dark. Use more fabrics if you wish.

CUTTING: Templates begin on page 96. For Feathered Star II use **A, A1, B, I, K, M, N,** and **P.** Instructions are given assuming bias-strip piecing will be used for the feather units.

For one 18 1/2'' Feathered Star II, cut these pieces:
Template **A:** 56 bias-cut units
      A1: 16 light
      B: 8 dark
      I: 8 dark
      K: 8 light
      M: 4 light
      N: 4 light
      P: 1 dark

---

3. Make four C units. Sew **A1** triangles to **B** diamonds as shown. Four of these units will be the reverse of the other four. Complete the feather rows, using **A** bias-cut feather units and **A** squares if called for. Sew the feather rows to **N** corner square.

Make 4 each   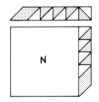

Unit C: Make 4

4. Sew A, B, and C units together in rows as shown. Sew long seams to join the rows. Complete halfway seams last.

Sew remaining portions of these seams last.

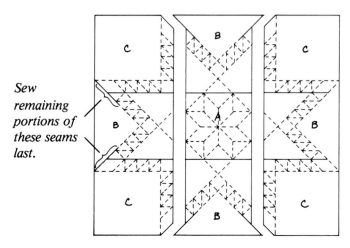

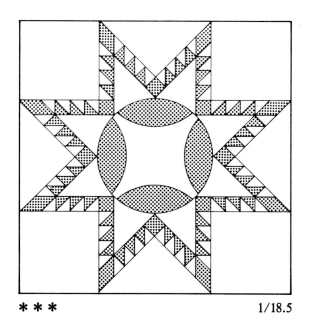

✳ ✳ ✳   1/18.5

FEATHERED STAR WITH REEL CENTER

18 1/2" block

The circular center on this block is fairly traditional. A similar block in an antique quilt is pictured on page 24. Refer to page 59 for help with piecing curves.

COLOR: Instructions here are written for a two-color design. Add more fabrics if you wish.

CUTTING: Templates for this block begin on page 96. Use **A, A1, B, J, M, N, O,** and **Q.** Cutting notations are given, assuming bias-strip piecing will be used for the feather units.

For one 18 1/2" Feathered Star With Reel Center, cut these pieces:

Template **A:** 48 bias-cut units, 8 dark squares

     A1: 16 light

     B: 8 dark

     J: 8 light

     M: 4 light

     N: 4 light

     O: 1 light

     Q: 4 dark

PIECING

1. Unit A, the star center, is called a Reel. Using curved seam techniques, sew the four **Q** pieces to the central **O** piece.

Unit A: Center

Make 1

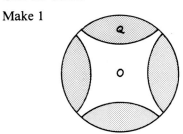

2. Make four B units. Make feather rows as shown, using **A** bias-cut units, **A1** triangles, and **A** squares. Attach feather rows to **M** triangles with halfway seams. Add **J** shapes.

Unit B: Make 4

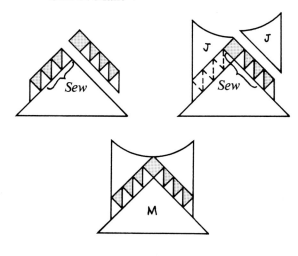

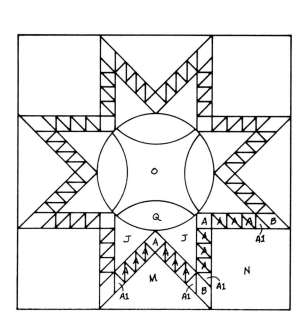

3. Make four C units. Sew **A1** triangles to **B** diamonds as shown. Four of these units will be the reverse of the other four. Complete the feather rows, using **A** bias-cut feather units and **A** squares. Sew the feather rows to **N** corner square.

Make 4 each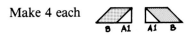

Unit C: Make 4

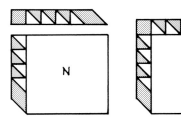

4. Sew B and C units together, then set the center A unit in. Complete halfway seams last.

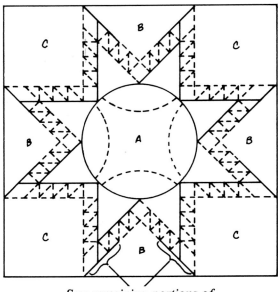

Sew remaining portions of these seams last.

TEMPLATES

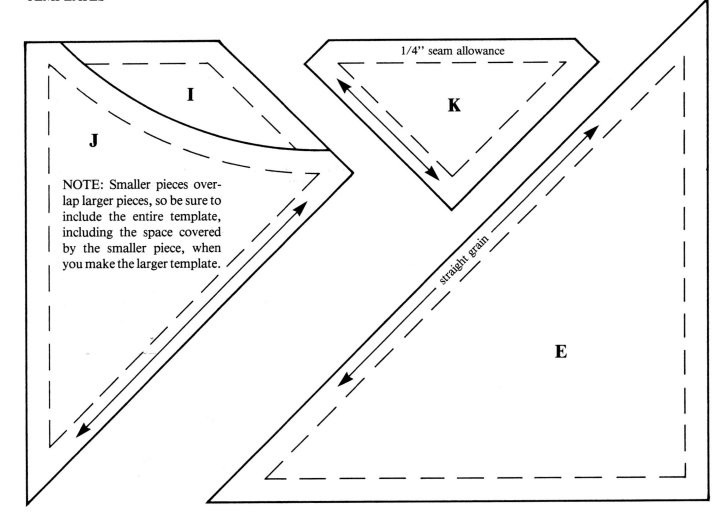

NOTE: Smaller pieces overlap larger pieces, so be sure to include the entire template, including the space covered by the smaller piece, when you make the larger template.

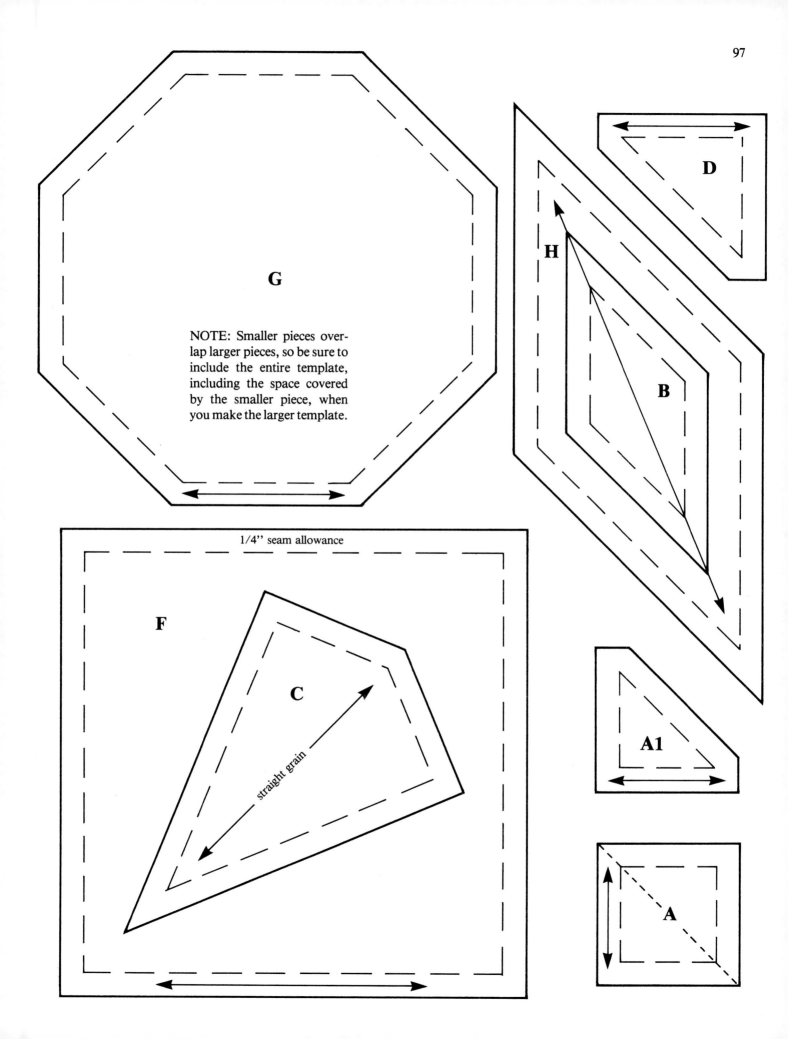

G

NOTE: Smaller pieces over-lap larger pieces, so be sure to include the entire template, including the space covered by the smaller piece, when you make the larger template.

D

H

B

1/4" seam allowance

F

C

straight grain

A1

A

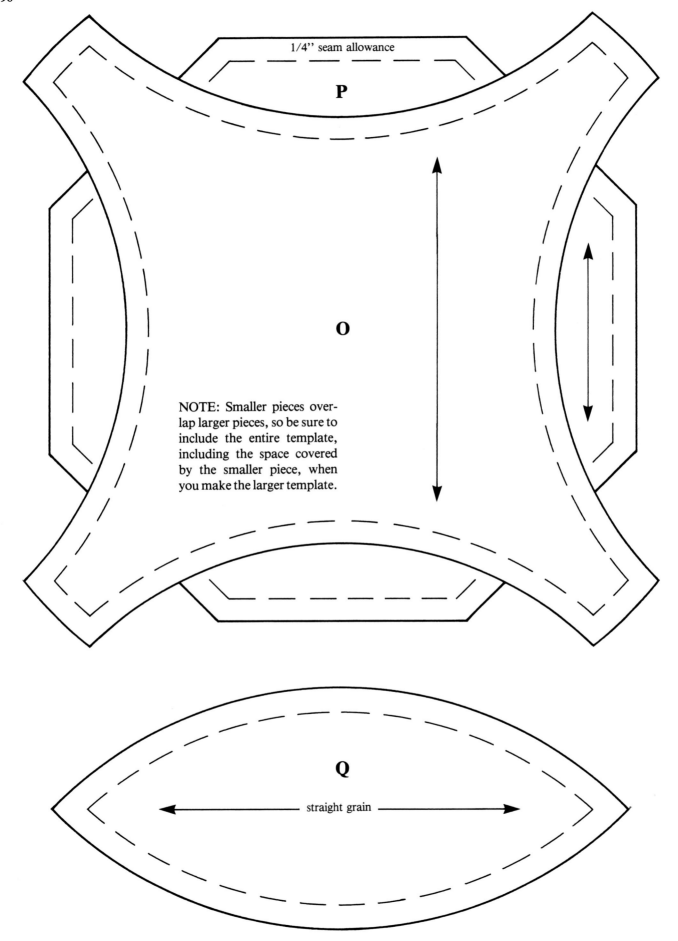

1/4'' seam allowance

P

O

NOTE: Smaller pieces overlap larger pieces, so be sure to include the entire template, including the space covered by the smaller piece, when you make the larger template.

Q

straight grain

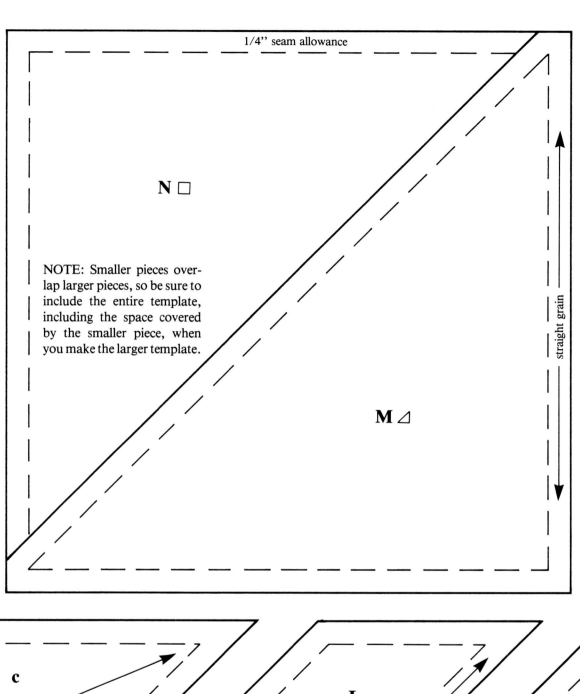

1/4" seam allowance

N □

NOTE: Smaller pieces over-lap larger pieces, so be sure to include the entire template, including the space covered by the smaller piece, when you make the larger template.

M △

straight grain

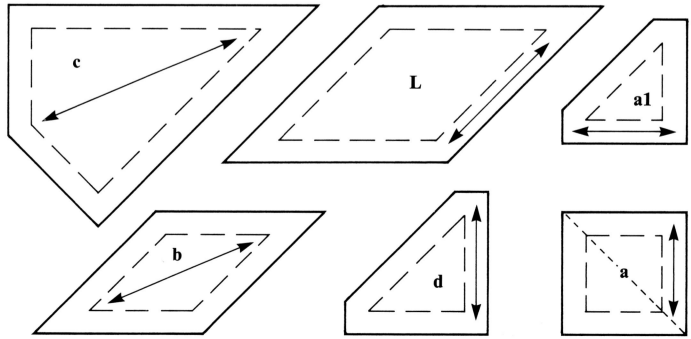

c

L

a1

b

d

a

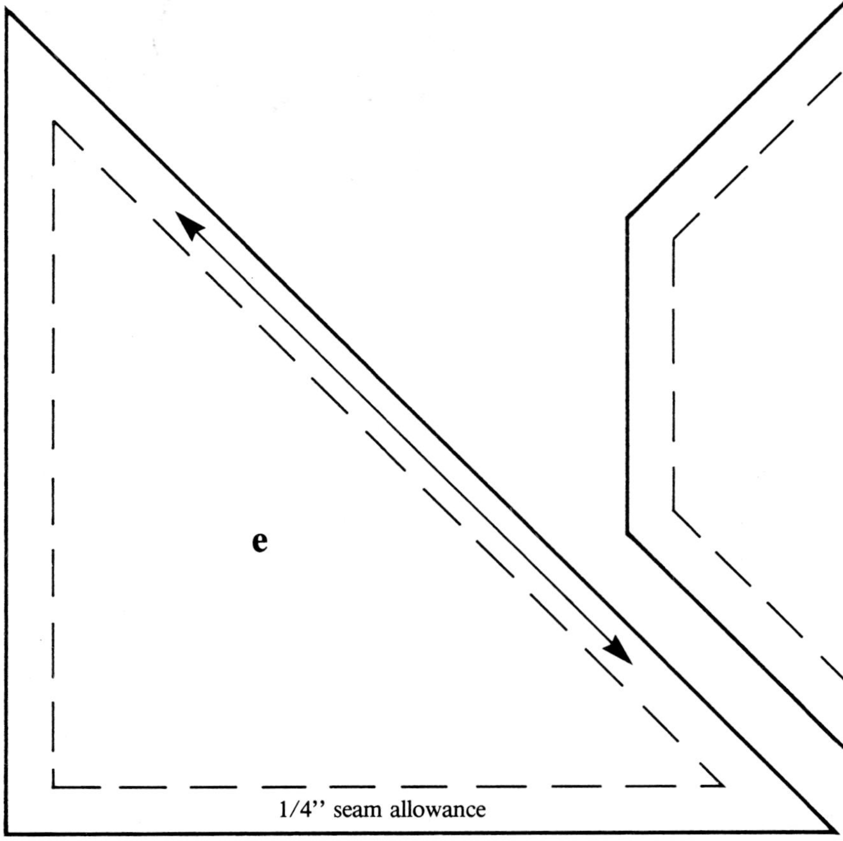

e

g

1/4'' seam allowance

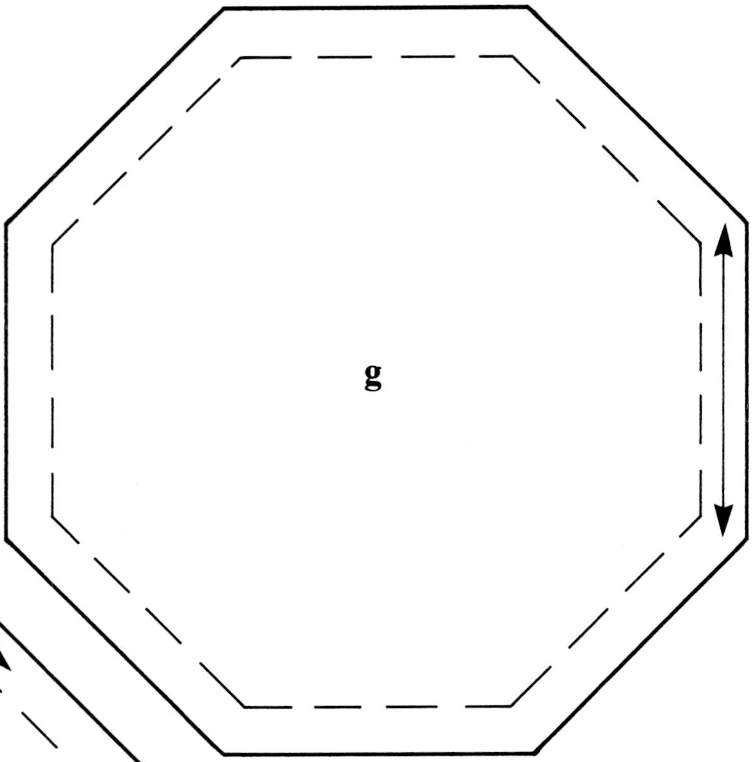

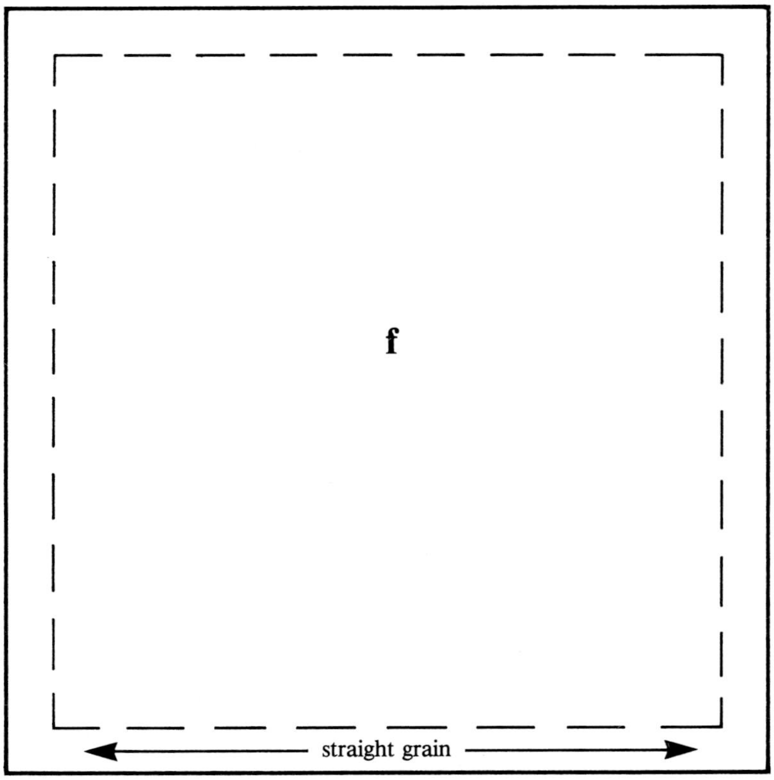

f

h

straight grain

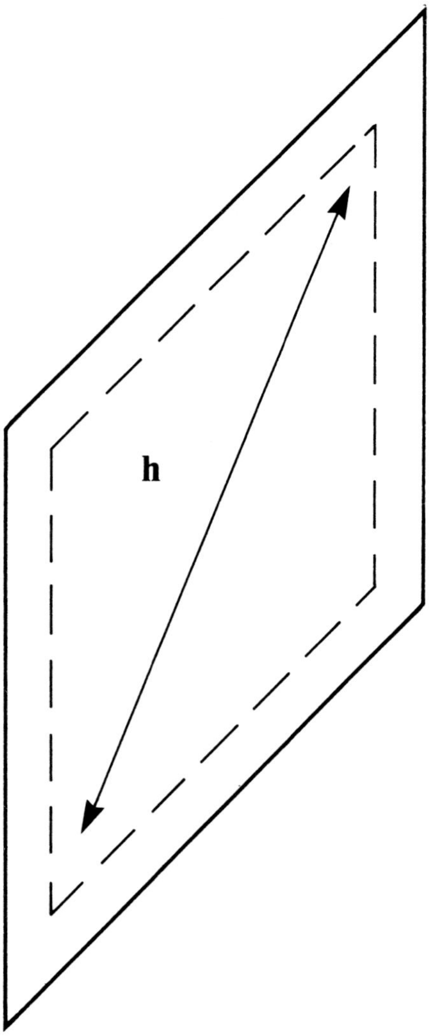

FEATHERED STAR QUILT PLANS

FEATHERED STAR WITH PINEAPPLE BORDER

Inspired by the 1850s crib quilt pictured on page 25, the top of this quilt takes only ten hours to cut and machine-piece, using the bias-strip method outlined on page 56 to make the feathers.

DIMENSIONS: 65" x 65"

MATERIALS: 45" wide yardage

Large-scale prints cut randomly work well in this quilt design.

Print A: 3 yds. (1/2 yd. for bias cuts, 2 yds. for #4 Border, and 1/2 yd. for other piecing)

Print B: 1 7/8 yds. (for Borders #1, #3, and 7 1/2 yds. of binding cut 1 1/2" wide)

Muslin: 2 yds. (1/2 yd. for bias cuts. 1 1/2 yds. for Border #2 and other piecing)

Backing: 4 yds.

Batting, thread, etc. to finish

DIRECTIONS:

1. Cut and set aside 1/2 yd. each of Print A and muslin for bias-strip piecing.

2. Set aside 2 yds. of Print A for Border #4.

3. From Print B, cut eight strips 3 1/4" wide (includes seam allowance) from the lengthwise grain of the fabric. These strips will be Border #1 and Border #3. Set aside. The remaining portion of Print B will be used for bias binding.

4. From 1 1/2 yds. remaining muslin, cut four strips 3 1/4" wide (includes seam allowance) for Border #2. Set aside.

5. Cut and piece Feathered Star center block of Print A and muslin. Templates and piecing instructions for this block are on page 60.

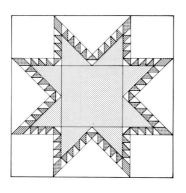

6. Add Borders #1, #2, and #3. These strips were cut previously. You may choose mitered or straight-sewn corners.

7. Cut and sew pieced Pineapple border sections (templates are on page 103) and sew to center section as shown.

    a. Make 16 pieced units. For each unit cut these pieces:
      Template #12: 9 bias-cut units (144 for whole quilt)
         #13: 2 muslin (32 in all)
         #11: 1 print (16 in all)

    Pieced border unit:
    Make 16

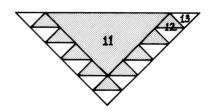

b. To complete border, cut twelve #10 of muslin and four #14 (for this template, use #10 and place on fold indicated). Join pieced units with muslin triangles and sew to center of quilt top as shown.

8. Cut four 10'' wide (includes seam allowance) strips for Border #4 from the remaining 2 yds. of Print A and sew to quilt. Choose either straight-sewn or mitered corners.

9. Add batting and backing. Quilt and finish edges with bias binding made from Print B.

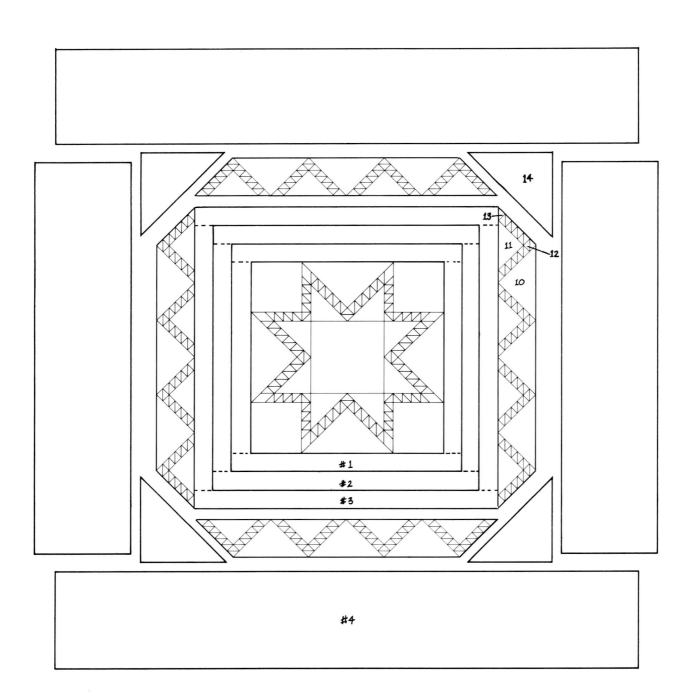

PINEAPPLE BORDER TEMPLATES

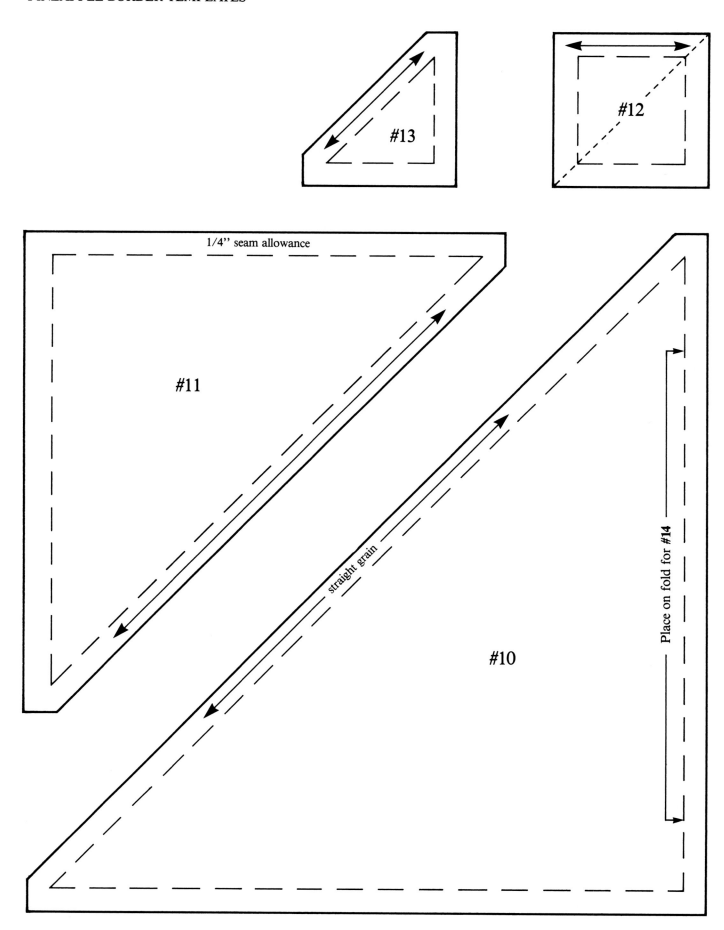

#13

#12

1/4'' seam allowance

#11

straight grain

#10

Place on fold for **#14**

STAR OF CHAMBLIE

Though traditional Feathered Star quilts are often worked in formal two or three color combinations, some of the most exciting versions are made of scraps. A scrap quilt made from this pattern is pictured on page 9. Instructions are given here for a many fabric quilt. You may use only two or three fabrics if you wish.

DIMENSIONS: 67 1/2" x 67 1/2"

MATERIALS: 45" wide yardage
- Print A: 2 1/2 yds. large scale print (such as paisley) for border
- Print B: 1/2 yd. plaid for lattices
- Print C: about 2 yds. total light print scraps
- Print D: about 2 yds. total dark print scraps
- Muslin: 1 yd.
- Backing: 4 1/4 yds.
- Binding: 8 1/4 yds. cut 1 1/2" wide from 3/4 yd. of dark print
- Batting, thread, etc. to finish

DIRECTIONS:

1. Cut four border strips 9" wide from the length of Print A. Set aside. Use leftover Print A in piecing blocks.

2. To make scrappy looking feathers using the bias-strip piecing method, cut 10" squares of nine different prints. Layer print squares with an equal number of 10" muslin squares. Cut into 2" wide bias strips and make the two-triangle feather units according to the bias-strip piecing instructions on page 56.

3. Make nine Star of Chamblie blocks. Instructions are on page 80.

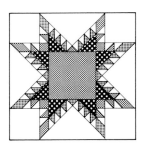

4. Cut 12 lattice pieces 3 1/2" x 15 1/2" of Print B.

5. Piece four 3" set blocks. Use extra **A** feather units and **A** squares cut from light prints.

6. Arrange Star of Chamblie blocks, lattice pieces, and set blocks in order on a flat surface to determine the best color balance. Sew the units together in rows. Trim lattices to fit the blocks exactly. Sew the rows together to make the quilt top.

7. Add borders of Print A with either straight-sewn or mitered corners.

8. Add batting and backing. Quilt and finish with bias binding.

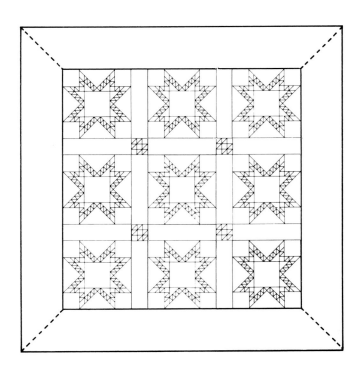

JOINING STARS

This quilt plan is for the twin-size quilt top pictured in color on page 28. The size can easily be changed by adding or subtracting rows of stars. The maker, Beverly Bynum, used many blue prints for the "feathers" in her quilt — you could choose to use only one fabric.

DIMENSIONS: 71" x 103"

MATERIALS: 45" wide fabric

    Print A: 3 yds. medium-scale pink print for two plain outer borders and piecing

    Print B: about 2 1/2 yds. total assorted medium blue prints for star "feathers" and sawtooth border

    Unbleached muslin or light solid: 6 yds.

    Backing: 6 yds.

    Bias binding: 10 yds. cut 1 1/2" wide from 7/8 yds. blue print

    Batting, thread, etc. to finish

DIRECTIONS

1. Cut 8 border strips 3" wide from the length of Print A. Set aside. Use leftover Print A for piecing blocks.

2. Set aside 2 1/2" yds. of muslin for bias-strip piecing. This will be used with the assorted blue prints to make the star "feathers" and the sawtooth border. See page 56 for bias-strip piecing instructions.

3. From the length of remaining muslin, cut two border strips 5 1/2" x 92" and two 5 1/2" x 62". Set aside. These border strips and those cut from Print A are longer than need be and will be trimmed to fit later. Use the remaining muslin for piecing.

4. Make 15 Joining Stars. Piecing instructions for the blocks and templates begin on page 76. This quilt, however, is not constructed in squares but as a bar quilt. It is pieced in sections that are joined in rows. The stars are formed when the completed rows are sewn together. For the whole quilt, cut these pieces:

    A: 360 bias-cut units of blue print and muslin

    A1: 120 muslin

    B: 180 bias-cut units of blue print and muslin

    B1: 120 muslin

    C: 60 pink Print A, R 60 pink Print A

    D: 180 pink Print A

    E: 16 muslin

    Ex2: 22 muslin

    M: 4 muslin

    Mx2: 12 muslin

    Mx4: 8 muslin

    O: 15 pink Print A (star center)

5. Make 22 A units.

Unit A

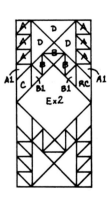

6. Make 16 B units.

Unit B

7. Sew A and B units together in rows as shown with cut pieces **E, Ex2, M, Mx2, Mx4,** and **O.** Make 2 of Row 1, 5 of Row 2, and 4 of Row 3.

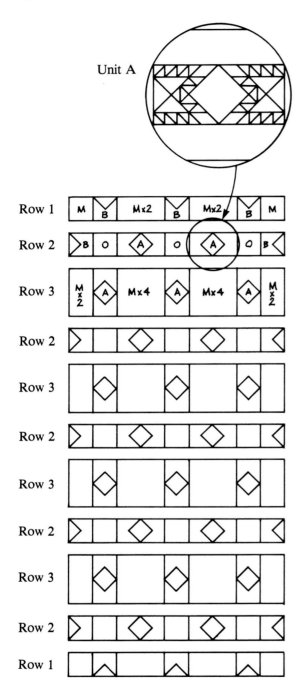

Unit A

Row 1
Row 2
Row 3
Row 2
Row 3
Row 2
Row 3
Row 2
Row 3
Row 2
Row 1

8. Sew the rows together to complete the center section of the quilt top.

9. Add 5 1/2" muslin inner border. Use straight-sewn or mitered corners.

10. Add the 3" Print A inner border. Use straight-sewn or mitered corners.

11. Cut and piece sawtooth border. With bias-strip piecing, make 232 two-triangle squares of blue prints and muslin. Use the template shown here. Construct the border sections as shown and sew to quilt top.

12. Add the 3" Print A outer border. Use straight-sewn or mitered corners.

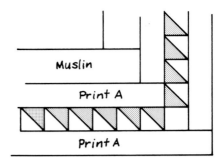

13. Press quilt top and mark quilting lines. Bar construction provides large unseamed spaces for fine quilting; take advantage of the opportunity.

14. Prepare backing and baste together with top and batting.

15. Hand quilt.

16. Bind with 1 1/2" bias binding made from blue print.

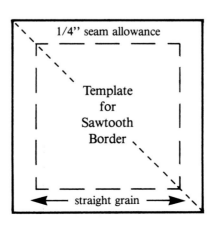

1/4" seam allowance

Template
for
Sawtooth
Border

← straight grain →

TWINKLING STAR WALL QUILT

This delicate pastel wall quilt could easily be made larger by adding more blocks. Notice the secondary designs that appear where the blocks are joined. A color photo appears on page 43.

DIMENSIONS: 28" x 28"

MATERIALS: 45" wide fabric

This is primarily a scrapbag project. Small amounts of ten different fabrics were used in the example pictured. Each block contains a "dark" pastel fabric, a "light" pastel, and muslin.

> Pastel prints: about 1 yd. total assorted (4 "dark," 4 "light," plus one other)
> Muslin: 1/2 yd.
> Backing: 1 yd.
> Binding: 3 1/4 yds. bias binding cut 1 1/2" wide from 1/2 yd. pastel print
> Batting, thread, etc. to finish

DIRECTIONS:

1. Cut and piece four 10" Twinkling Star blocks of pastel fabrics and muslin. Instructions and templates begin on page 89 and are written for two colors. The blocks in this wall quilt have three colors. Use muslin and the "dark" pastel prints to make bias-cut units with Templates #1 and #4. Use the "light" pastel prints for Templates #2 and #4.

5. Press quilt top and mark for quilting.

6. Prepare backing and baste together with batting and quilt top.

7. Hand quilt.

8. Bind with bias binding cut 1 1/2" wide from pastel fabric.

2. Arrange pieced blocks for color and set them together as shown. Match the triangle points carefully.

3. For inner border, cut 4 strips of a light pastel fabric 1 1/2" x 24". Sew to quilt center with either straight-sewn or mitered corners. Trim excess.

4. For outer border, cut 4 strips 3 1/2" x 22 1/2". Sew to previous piecing, incorporating the 4 cornerstones (use template on page 112) as shown.

FEATHERED STAR SAMPLER QUILT

This sampler utilizes five of the eight 12" Feathered Star blocks offered in the pattern section. Substitute other designs than these or add more blocks to make the quilt larger. A color photo of this quilt appears on page 13.

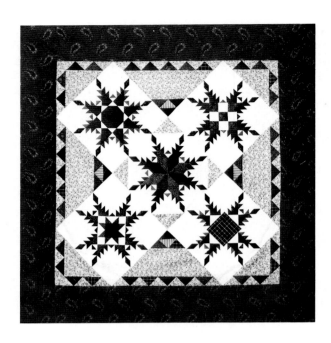

DIMENSIONS: 44" x 44"

MATERIALS: 45" wide fabric
Navy print: 1 3/8 yds. for border and piecing, plus about 1/3 yd. total assorted other navy prints
Turkey red prints: about 1/2 yd. total assorted
Medium navy print: 1/2 yd.
Muslin: 1 yd.
Backing: 1 3/8 yds.
Binding: 5 yds. bias-cut 1 1/2" wide from 1/2 yd. navy or red print
Batting, thread, etc. to finish

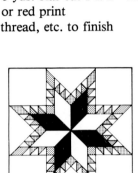

Feathered Le Moyne Star

Radiant Star

DIRECTIONS

1. Cut 4 border strips 5 1/2" wide from the length of the dark navy print. Set aside. These pieces are longer than need be and will be trimmed to fit later.

2. Cut and piece five 12" Feathered Star blocks. Choose from the eight blocks offered in the pattern section. The designs used in the example pictured here are the 12" Feathered Le Moyne Star on page 91 (To make this block as pictured here, replace the four light corner squares with squares pieced of triangle **e.** Cut 4 light and 4 medium navy.), the 12" Feather Star With Nine-Patch Center on page 79, the 12" Feather Star With Morning Star Center on page 78, the 12" Joining Star on page 76, and the 12" Radiant Star on page 92. Refer to these page numbers for piecing instructions and templates.

*Feather Star With
Nine-Patch Center*

*Feather Star With
Morning Star Center*

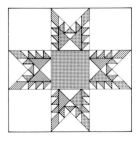

Joining Star

3. Cut and piece the triangular side sections (A and B) that complete the quilt set. Make 4 section A and 4 section B. Use templates #1, #2, and #3 beginning on page 112. Cut these pieces:

> Template #1: 48 dark navy and turkey red prints
> 52 medium navy
> #2: 4 medium navy
> #3: 4 medium navy

Section A: Make 4

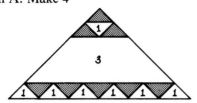

Section B: Make 4

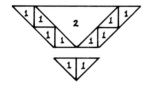 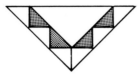

4. Set the A and B sections together with the five pieced blocks as shown.

5. Add navy borders. Use straight-sewn or mitered corners. Trim excess.

6. Press quilt top and mark for quilting.

7. Prepare backing and baste together with batting and quilt top.

8. Hand quilt.

9. Bind with bias strips cut 1 1/2" wide from 1/2 yd. navy turkey red print.

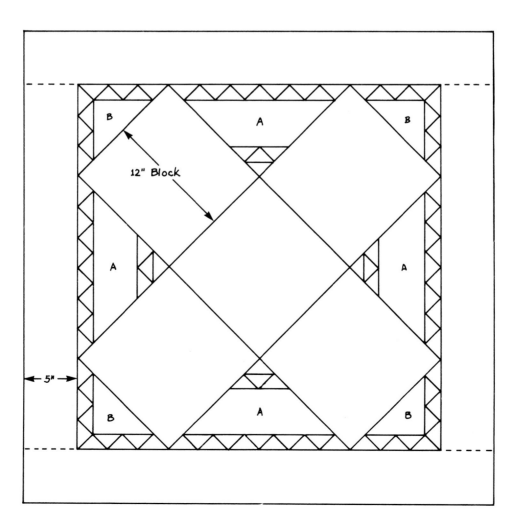

CHRISTMAS RADIANT STAR BANNER

The Radiant Star is one of the prettiest and easiest to piece of the Feathered Star designs. It looks smashing in red and green, so why not make a holiday banner to brighten your home or give as a gift? A color photo appears on page 36.

DIMENSIONS: 21" x 51"

MATERIALS: 45" wide fabric
   Dark green solid: 1/4 yd.
   Red prints: about 1/4 yd. total assorted
   Green prints: about 1/4 yd. total assorted
   Dark green print: 1 5/8 yds. for backing and borders
   Muslin: 1/4 yd.
   Binding: 4 1/8 yds. bias cut 1 1/2" wide from 1/2 yd. of
         red or green print
   Batting, thread, etc. to finish

DIRECTIONS:

1. Make three 15" Radiant Star blocks. Instructions and templates begin on page 92. The colors for the blocks in this banner have been placed differently than in the instruction on page 92, so instead, for each block, cut these pieces:

   Template **A:** 32 bias-cut units of dark green and muslin,
         8 red squares
   A1: 16 dark green
   B: 8 muslin
   C: 8 green print
   D: 8 light
   E: 4 green print, 4 red print, 4 dark green
      print
   G: 1 red

Color placement:

Unit A

Unit B

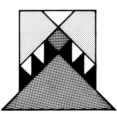

Unit C

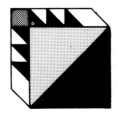

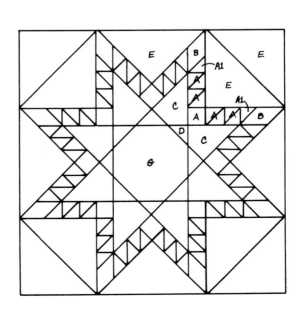

2. Set the three pieced blocks together as shown.

3. Cut border strips 3 1/2'' wide from length of dark green print. Sew to center pieced section. Use straight-sewn or mitered corners.

4. Press quilt top and mark for quilting.

5. Use remaining dark green print for backing and baste together with batting and quilt top.

6. Hand quilt.

7. Bind with bias strips cut 1 1/2'' wide from 1/2 yd. of green or red print.

VARIATIONS:

The three small projects sketched here can also be made with 15'' Radiant Star blocks. Use block Template **E,** and Templates #9 and #10 on page 113 to complete the borders.

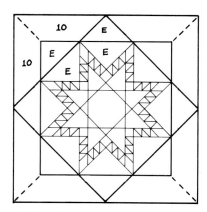

Wall Quilt

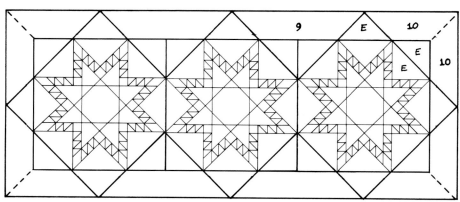

Banner

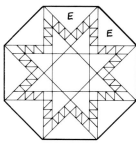

Table Mat

TEMPLATES

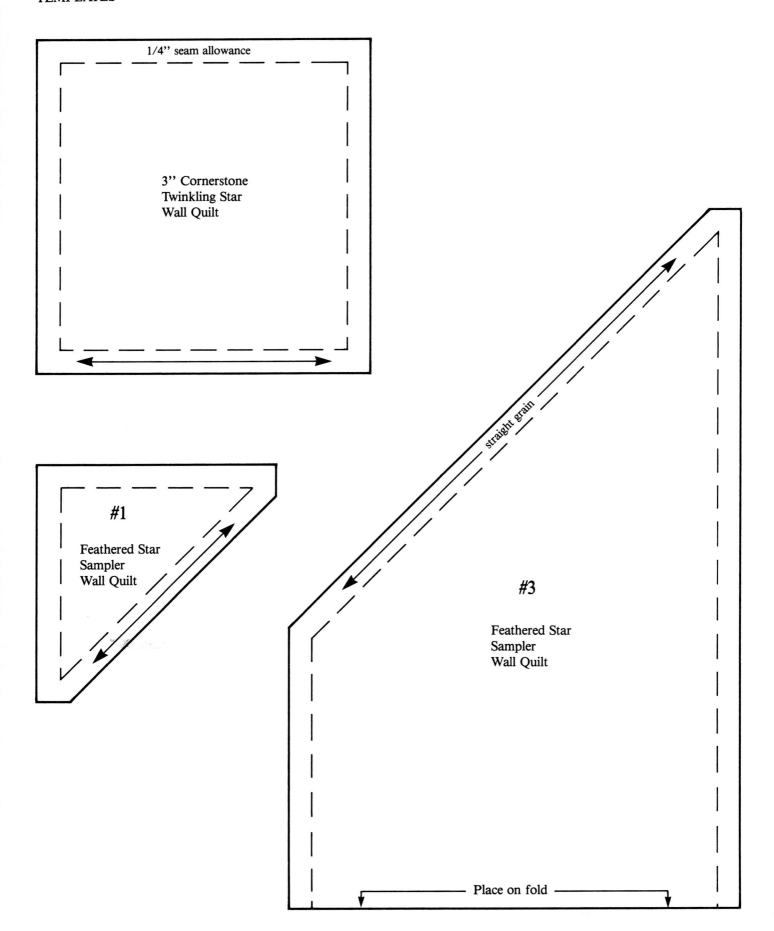

1/4" seam allowance

3" Cornerstone
Twinkling Star
Wall Quilt

#1

Feathered Star
Sampler
Wall Quilt

straight grain

#3

Feathered Star
Sampler
Wall Quilt

Place on fold

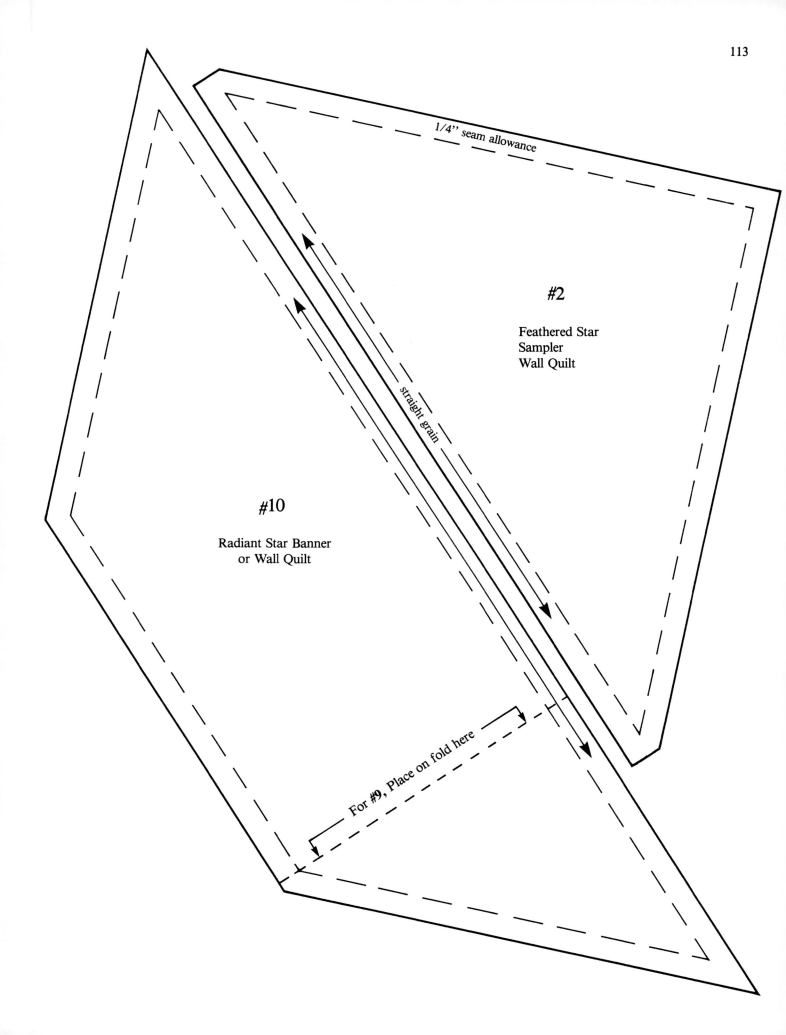

1/4'' seam allowance

#2

Feathered Star
Sampler
Wall Quilt

straight grain

#10

Radiant Star Banner
or Wall Quilt

For #9, Place on fold here

DRAFTING THE FEATHERED STAR

Variable Star

Sawtooth Star

Le Moyne Star

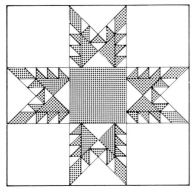

Joining Star   *1/16*

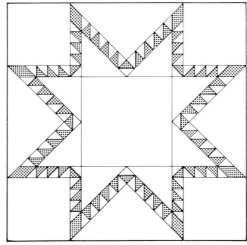

Feathered Star   *1/21.25*

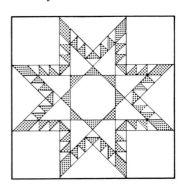

Radiant Star   *1/15*

There are twenty patterns for Feathered Star blocks in this book, but some readers, no doubt, will see a Feathered Star design in a gallery or elsewhere and want to make it. This section on drafting is for the quilter who is not satisfied with using a printed pattern, who wants to know "how" and "why," and who will go on to design new and original blocks in sizes different than those presented here.

The purpose of the drafting section is to give you, the creator of quilts, the tools and skills to design and draft new and original Feathered Star blocks. By actually doing these drafting exercises, you will gain important knowledge about the stars that I simply do not have the words or the space to tell you. You will know where to start and where to go from there. You will learn how important it is to draw lines accurately. You will see new designs in your drawings as you work. You will think, "Well, if this works this way, then what if . . . ." and the process will be working. Drafting lets you get inside a design and truly know it. It is one of my favorite things about quiltmaking.

What follows is the bare bones of my Feathered Star drafting class. In it, I guide students through three basic draftings, exploring concepts and building vocabulary as we go.

If you want to follow along and do the draftings, you will need these supplies and tools:

> 17" x 22" sheets of 1/4" and 1/8" graph paper
> Sharp pencil and eraser
> C-Thru B-85 ruler (2" x 18" with 1/8" red grid)
> Bow compass with 7" radius
> Colored Pencils

Geometry and Block Size

There are three basic eight-pointed geometric stars in patchwork. Border the points of any of these stars with rows of tiny triangles, and a Feathered Star design is created. Two of these basic stars are drafted on grids and are very similar: the Sawtooth Star, based on a sixteen-square grid, and the Variable Star, based on a nine-square grid. The third star is the Le Moyne Star, which is not based on a grid, but on a circle. It has 45 degree diamonds and is easily identified by its equidistant points.

Each of the following draftings involve adding feathers to a basic geometric star. Now, usually when one drafts a patchwork design, the outside of the square is drawn first, and other lines are added on the inside to make the pattern. It is difficult, though not impossible, to draft a Feathered Star with that approach. I have found it easiest to draft Feathered Stars from the inside out. No matter what the design variation, I start with the size or measurement of the smallest triangles or "feathers" and draft the block accordingly. I rarely know how big the block will be until it is drawn. In most cases, the finished size of the block is not that important anyway — the quilt is simply designed around it.

Sometimes a specific block dimension is needed. Once a block is drafted in one size, it only takes a bit of simple algebra to change the finished size to another dimension. The equation explained in the next paragraph is based on a ratio or proportion. Each Feathered Star design has its own specific ratio of the size of the feathers to the size of the finished block. The fraction below each block drawing in the pattern section denotes its ratio. Size changes for the blocks can be made using these numbers.

EXAMPLE: The basic Feathered Star block for my red and white sampler is drafted on a 1'' scale, which means the smallest triangles or feathers measure 1''. The finished block measures 16''. When you compare the two measurements (feather to finished block), it is called a ratio and can be expressed as a fraction 1/16, which is read 1 is to 16. What if you want to make the same design in a 12'' size? The question now is how big the feathers should be. Let x represent the feather dimension in the 12'' block. You can write a simple equation:

$$1/16 = x/12 \quad (1 \text{ is to } 16 \text{ as } x \text{ is to } 12)$$
which is solved like this: $16x = 12$
$$x = 12/16$$
$$x = 3/4$$

The feathers in your 12'' block design must measure 3/4''. Redraft the star, starting with 3/4'' triangles instead of 1'' triangles.

The size of a block can also be changed by changing the size of the feathers (e.g., from 1'' to 3/4''), or by changing the number of feathers (from three to four or five) on a side.

Drafting Tips

1. Use the most accurate graph paper you can find. Check it to make sure it is true. Some papers will be accurate in one direction but not the other. Find a store that sells supplies to drafting or engineering students. The large sheets (17'' x 22'') come in several grids — 1/4'', 1/5'', 1/6'', 1/8'', and 1/10''. I like to keep some of each on hand so I'll have it when I need it. If you can, buy the kind with the heavy lines at the 1'' increments — it is easier to work with. Expect to pay from 25¢ to 85¢ per sheet.

2. Use a sharp pencil. Never draft in ink — it can't be erased. A fine tipped mechanical drawing pencil is ideal, but an ordinary #2 pencil with a good sharpener will do just fine. Keep your pencil sharp. Drawn lines have width, especially ones made with dull pencils and make draftings inaccurate.

3. Be aware that clear plastic grid rulers are not always printed accurately. Some rulers vary up to 1/16'' from a true 1/4'' along the long sides. Check your ruler to see if it is accurate. I still like and use a clear plastic ruler for drafting because of its size, the printed grid that gives you parallel lines, and the fact that you can see through it.

In general, you will have to place your ruler a short distance from where you want to locate a line. If the edge of the ruler is exactly on the line, the line you draw with the pencil will be in the wrong place.

4. Obtain a good compass. A compass is used for two things: drawing circles and arcs, and taking (and keeping) measurements. The dimestore variety is not good enough; it slips. A bow compass with a 7'' radius and a roller stop to hold a setting is sufficient for most operations encountered while drafting patchwork patterns. Occasionally (but not for quilts in this book), an extension for the bow compass or a bar compass will be needed for larger settings. Use fine sandpaper to keep the lead sharp.

5. Real geometric terms are used in the drafting exercises, so you might find a quick read-through of a tenth-grade geo-

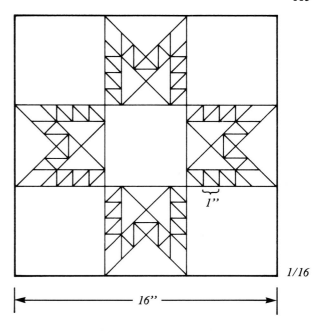

1/16

16''

metry text or basic mechanical drawing book helpful. Other books that deal with drafting patchwork patterns are *Patchwork Patterns* by Jinny Beyer and *Patchworkbook* by Judy Martin — both are excellent.

How to Bisect a Line Using a Compass

To divide any line in half, set your compass at about three-fourths of the line's length (more than half, less than whole). Place the point of the compass at one end of the line and strike two arcs, one above and one below the line. Repeat the process from the other end of the line. The drawn arcs should cross and will make two points, one above and one below the line. Connect these two points with a line. It will be perpendicular to the original line and will cross it at the midpoint, dividing it into two equal sections.

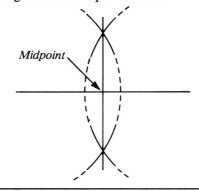

Midpoint

Decimal Equivalents

.1 = 1/10	.333 = 1/3	.666 = 2/3
.125 = 1/8	.375 = 3/8	.7 = 7/10
.166 = 1/6	.4 = 2/5	.75 = 3/4
.2 = 1/5	.5 = 1/2	.8 = 4/5
.25 = 1/4	.6 = 3/5	.833 = 5/6
.3 = 3/10	.625 = 5/8	.875 = 7/8

Variable Star

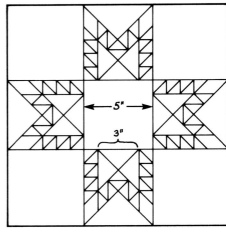

Joining Star   *1/16*

DRAFTING I: JOINING STAR

The first drafting is of a Joining Star. This drafting is drawn on a large sheet of 1/4'' graph paper. I use a 1'' scale — the smallest dimension in the block — so the feathers will be 1'' triangles. At this point, you do not know how big the finished block will be, but you do know that the feather measures 1'' on its short side.

You will not be drawing the whole Feathered Star design. Only those parts of the design necessary to make templates need be drawn.

This simple drafting is of a Feathered Star that is based on the nine-square grid Variable Star. It is the basic star for my red and white Feathered Star Sampler shown on page 12. Like the other Feathered Star draftings, once the basic star is drawn, design changes, such as substituting different centers or changing the block orientation, can be made easily.

Study the block. Look at the feathers. There are three 1'' feathers along the long side of a larger triangle. Therefore, that line, the hypotenuse, must be 3'' long. An identical triangle sits next to it, so the hypotenuse of that triangle also must be 3'' long. A row of 1'' feathers lies on both sides of this 3'' dimension. So add 1 + 3 + 1 = 5. Five inches, then, is the length of the side of the center square.

1. Draw a 5'' square (Template #1) and extend its sides. To extend a line simply means to make it longer. At this point you do not know how long these lines need to be. It is all right to make them too long; unnecessary parts can be erased later.

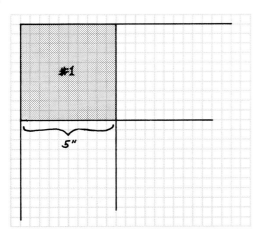

2. Draw lines 1'' inside of and parallel to the extended lines as shown.

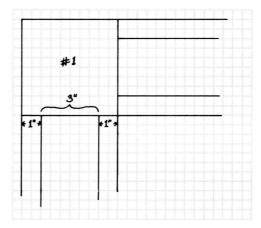

3. In this 1'' wide column, draw three 1'' squares. Divide the squares in half on the diagonal to make feather units (Template #3).

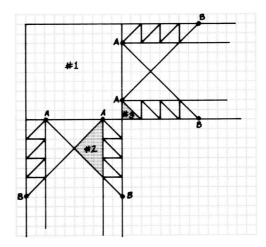

4. Draw diagonal lines that begin at the A points and end at the B points as shown. The large triangles thus created are Template #2.

5. The feathers that fit along the short side of the #2 triangle will be a different size than Template #3. To draw these new feathers, find the midpoint of the short sides of the #2 triangles as shown. On 1/4'' graph paper, that line passes diagonally across six 1/4'' squares. Simply count down three (half of the six) diagonal squares; that will be the center. (When drafting this star in other sizes, counting squares to find the midpoint may not work. (See "How to Bisect a Line Using a Compass" on page 115.) Using the graph paper as a guide, draw diagonal lines that begin at the midpoints and run parallel to the short sides of the #2 triangles. The square thus formed is Template #4. The parallelogram at the tip is Template #5. Draw two more #4 size squares as shown and divide them in half to make feather Template #6.

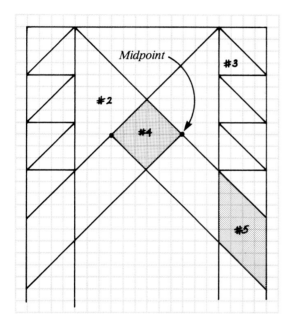

6. The side triangle (Template #7) is made by connecting the tips of the #5 parallelograms.

7. The corner square (Template #8) measures 5 1/2'' on each side and can be completely drawn from that dimension.

To get the finished size of the block, add 5 1/2'' + 5'' + 5 1/2'' = 16''

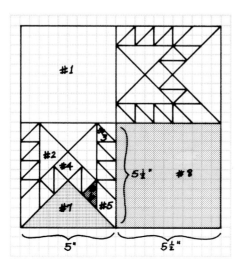

Variations of the Joining Star can be made by changing the center in a number of ways.

You can also change it by altering the orientation and outline of the block. The resulting star pictured here is called the Star of Chamblie and is the block used in the scrap quilt shown on page 9. Further changes in this block could be made by applying the above center suggestions.

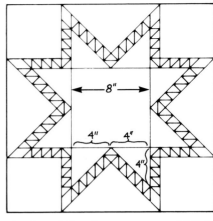

Sawtooth Star

Feathered Star I   *1/21.25*

DRAFTING II:
FEATHERED STAR I

This drafting is also drawn on a large sheet of 1/4'' graph paper. Again, begin with a 1'' feather dimension.

Notice that there are four feathers or four equal divisions along the short side of the triangle which is the leg of a large base star. Since these will be 1'' segments, the side of the large triangle must measure 4''. This triangle is a right isosceles triangle, which is defined as a triangle having a 90-degree angle and two equal sides. If one of these sides measures 4'', then so must the other. Two 4'' triangles fit along the center square, so the length of the side of that square must be 8''. A square has four equal sides, so if you know the length of one side, you can draw the whole square.

1. Begin by drawing an 8'' square. This center square can be used as a design space or left plain. In the block on page 62, a Variable Star is featured. You could use any sort of design you wish.

2. Next, extend the sides of the center square at least 6''.

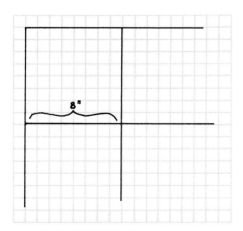

8'' square with sides extended

3. On each extended line, measure out 4'' (this is the length of one side of the large triangle) and make a dot. Draw diagonal lines that begin at the midpoint of the side of the center square and pass through the 4'' marks on the extended lines. Let these new lines go beyond the extended lines about 1 1/2''. Now there should be an 8'' center square (Template #1) and four 4'' triangles (Template #2).

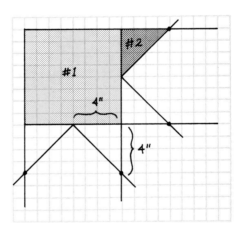

4. In the lower right section of the drawing, add feathers along the 4'' sides of the #2 triangles. Since the dimension of the feathers is to be 1'', draw two lines, each 1'' out from and parallel to the sides of the #2 triangles. A 1'' square (Template #3) will appear where the lines cross.

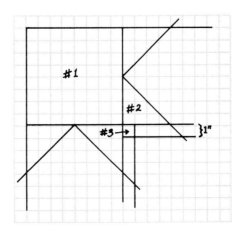

5. Draw three more 1″ squares along each large triangle as shown. Divide each 1″ square in half on the diagonal to form two equal 1″ triangles. Template #4 is a single triangle at the end of the row of divided squares.

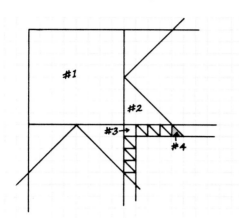

6. The next step is to add feathers along the long side of the #2 triangle. This is where many template makers run into geometric difficulties. It soon becomes apparent that the templates used for feathers along the short side of the large triangle will not fit evenly along the long side in the sawtooth configuration. To understand why, return to tenth grade and plane geometry.

The formula used to find the hypotenuse (the long side) of a right isosceles triangle is $s\sqrt{2}$, which means you multiply the short side of the triangle by $\sqrt{2}$. The square root of two ($\sqrt{2}$) is 1.414 which is rounded-off decimal. You can round it off further to 1.4. Going to the 4″ triangle (#2) you can apply the formula:

$$4'' \times 1.4 = 5.6''$$

Five and sixth-tenths inches is the length of the hypotenuse of this triangle. Now, 5.6″ is not evenly divisible by 1″, the size of our feather template, #4. Therefore, a different size template will be needed if sawtooth feathers are to fit properly in that space.

Think now about the 4″ triangle, #2. Four 1″ feathers (Template #4) fit along the short side of #2, and the length of the hypotenuse is 5.6″, which is not divisible by 1″. The #4 template will not fit here. You need to find a feather size that is as close to 1″ as possible (so the feather sizes are not obviously different) and will divide evenly into 5.6″. Try 5.

$$5.6 \div 5 = 1.12''$$

1.12″ is very close to 1.125″ which, if you know your decimal equivalents (there is a table on page 115), is 1 1/8″. This dimension, then, is sufficiently close to 1″ so the casual observer should not be able to see that two sizes of feathers exist in the block.

The feathers that are to fit along the hypotenuse of the large triangle #2 will measure 1.12″. But how do you draw them? Now, 1.12″ cannot be measured accurately with a conventional ruler, so you can borrow a method from mechanical drawing to divide the 5.6″ line into five equal parts.

a. Draw a line (B) that begins at the midpoint of the 8″ center square and extends to the right exactly 5″. A 5″ line is

used because it is easily divisible by five, the desired number of divisions.

b. Divide line B into five equal sections by placing a mark at each 1″ increment.

c. Draw line C from the end of line A to the end of line B.

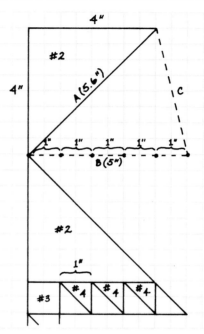

d. Carefully draw four more lines that are absolutely parallel (use the grid lines on the B-85 C-thru ruler) to line C and begin at the 1″ marks on line B. The four new lines will end on line A and divide it into equal sections. Each section should measure 1.12″. Check the accuracy of the sections first with a ruler; they should all measure just under 1 1/8″. Check them also with a compass by taking a setting from the first point on line A to the second, and then checking the other sections to that setting.

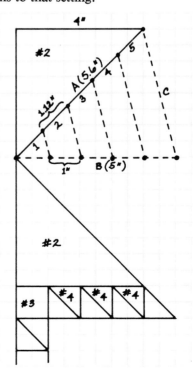

Once line A is divided, you need to draw the square feather units. Start with the most central small square. This square will give you the new feather template.

e. Let us call the midpoint of the side of the center square, point D and the first point on line A, point E. The distance between D and E is 1.12''. Set the compass to this distance. Place the point of the compass on D. Swing the compass lead down to lower line A and strike an arc. This new point is point F, and it is also 1.12'' from point D. DE = DF.

Move the compass point to E and strike an arc that crosses line B. Do the same from point F. Where these two arcs cross line B becomes point G. Points D, E, F, and G are the corner points of a square (Template #5), which is the base for the new feather template.

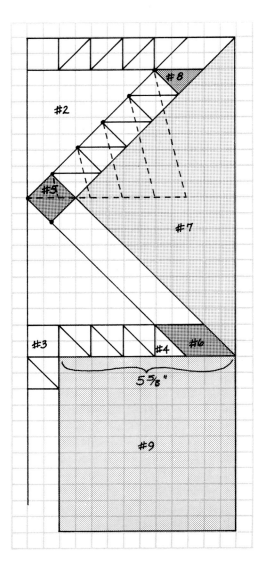

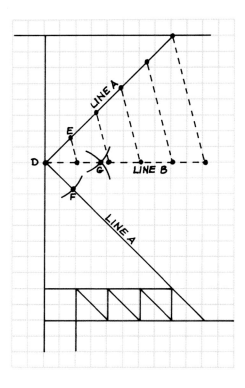

6. To make the row of feathers, draw a line as shown that begins at point E, passes through point G, and is absolutely parallel to lower line A. Draw a line from point F through point G that is parallel to upper line A. A square (Template #5) will appear where the two lines cross. Also, a parallelogram (Template #6), the tip of the star, will be completed. Draw four more squares along line A using the division points as guides. Divide each square in half on the diagonal to form triangles (Template #8).

7. The large side triangle (Template #7) is a right isosceles triangle with a 10'' base. Draw it by connecting the tips of the parallelograms on either side.

8. One side of the corner square (from the corner of Template #3 to the tip of the parallelogram, #6) measures 5 5/8''. So draw the corner square (Template #9) based on that dimension.

Two corner squares (5 5/8'' + 5 5/8'') plus the 10''-side triangle give a finished dimension of 21 1/4'' for the block.

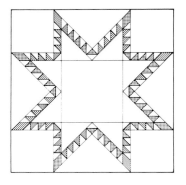

Le Moyne Star

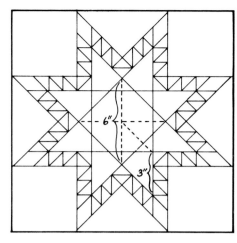

Radiant Star   1/15
Chestnut Burr

DRAFTING III:
THE RADIANT STAR

This drafting is based on the Le Moyne Star and is called a Radiant Star or Chestnut Burr. Aunt Martha's Catalog offered a pattern for a 12'' version of the Radiant Star for fifteen cents in 1932. It long has been a popular Feathered Star pattern because of its grace, and it is probably the easiest of all the stars to piece. This star has only one feather template, so you will not get the two sizes confused. It also has a true diamond at the tip instead of a parallelogram, which would have to be reversed half the time to fit properly.

The octagonal center of the Radiant Star is a fairly empty central space and can be embellished with quilting, applique, embroidery, or additional piecing. The circle drawn during drafting also could be used as a design space, as illustrated by the Feathered Star with Reel Center on page 95.

Draft the Radiant star on a large sheet of 1/8'' graph paper. Again, the feather size will be 1''. Study the block. Along the side of the kite shape that is the leg of this star, there are three equal divisions, three feathers. This line then, is 3'' long. Imagine that this 3'' line is one side of a 45-degree diamond (the Radiant Star, like the Le Moyne Star, has 45-degree diamonds in this space). Because all the sides of this diamond are equal, all the sides here must be 3'' long. Moving to the center of the square and then to the opposite corners, you will find a 6'' dimension.

1. Using the heavy lines on graph paper, draw two 6'' lines that bisect each other. Connect the ends of the lines to form a square.

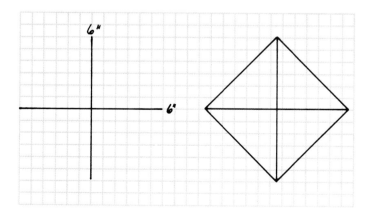

2. With your compass set at 3'', draw a circle that encloses the square. The circle should pass exactly through the corner points of the square.

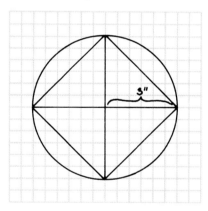

3. Draw two more 6'' lines that begin and end on the circle and pass through the center at exactly a 45-degree angle. Establish the 45-degree angle by making sure the line you draw passes exactly corner to corner across the little squares of the graph paper. Connect the ends of these lines to form a second square.

Two templates, the center octagon (Template #1) and the small triangle (Template #2) next to it, can now be identified. Because of all the lines in this drafting, it is easiest to find the templates if they are lightly shaded with colored pencils.

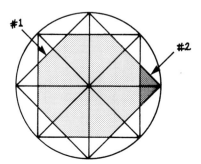

4. Extend the sides of both squares. Let the lines cross. Now you can find a new template, #3, which is kite-shaped. Check to make sure that the long sides of the kite measure exactly 3''.

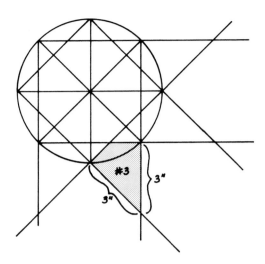

5. In what will be the lower right area of the block, draw two lines that are 1'' from and parallel to the extended lines. Where the two lines cross, a 1'' square (Template #4) will be formed. Draw in two more 1'' squares along each kite. Divide each square in half on the diagonal to make two equal triangles. The extra 1'' triangle at the end of the row will be designated as Template #5.

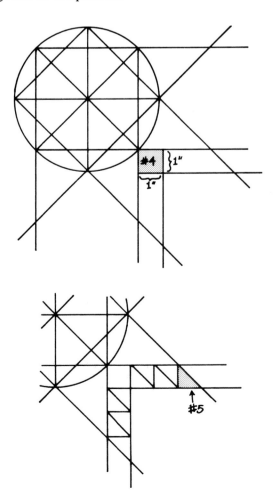

6. To make the diamond at the tip of the kite, you will need a compass. The length of one side of this diamond is the hypotenuse of the 1'' triangle, #5. Following the illustration, take a compass setting of AB. Swing the compass and strike an arc on line m creating point C. AB = AC. Without changing the setting, move the compass point to point B and strike an arc on line p, creating point D. Connect point C to point D. the figure just drawn is a 45-degree diamond with AB = AC = BD = AD — Template #6.

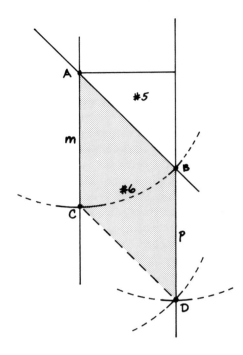

7. One side of the corner square is 4 3/8''; draw the shape based on that dimension. This is template #7.

8. The large side triangle (Template #8) is equal to half of the corner square, #7. To make that shape, simply divide the corner square in half on the diagonal.

The finished size of the block is 15''

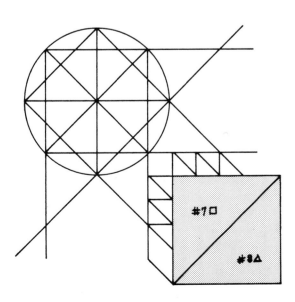

GLOSSARY OF TECHNIQUES

Tools and Supplies

Drawing Supplies: Graph paper in a 1/8" grid and colored pencils for drawing quilt plans and sketching design ideas.

Rulers: I use two rulers; both are clear plastic with a red grid of 1/8" squares. A short ruler is for drawing quilt designs on graph paper; a longer one, 2" wide and 18" long, is for drafting designs full size, making templates, and measuring and marking borders and quilting lines. If your local quilt shop doesn't carry them, try a stationery store or any place that carries drafting or art supplies. Another useful tool is a 12" plastic 45°/90° right angle.

Scissors: You will need scissors for paper, a good sharp pair for cutting fabric only, and possibly a little pair for snipping threads. If your fabric scissors are dull, have them sharpened. If they are close to "dead," invest in a new pair. It's worth it.

Template Material: To make templates, you will need graph paper or tracing paper, lightweight posterboard (manila file folders are good) or plastic, and a glue stick.

Markers: Most marking on fabric can be done with a regular #2 lead pencil and a white dressmaker's pencil. Keep them sharp. There is a blue felt-tip marking pen available that is water erasable; it works especially well for marking quilting designs. (When you no longer need the lines for guides, spray them with cool water and the blue marks will disappear.) Ask the salespeople at a local fabric or quilt shop about the different kinds of marking pens available.

Sewing Machine: It needn't be fancy. All you need is an evenly locking straight stitch. Whatever kind of sewing machine you have, get to know it and how it runs. If it needs servicing, have it done, or get out the manual and do it yourself. Replace the old needle with a new one. Often, if your machine has a zigzag stitch, it will have a throat plate with an oblong hole for the needle to pass through. You might want to replace this plate with one that has a little round hole for straight stitching. This will help eliminate problems you might have with the edges of fabrics being fed into the hole by the action of the feed dog.

Needles: A supply of new sewing machine needles for light to medium weight cottons is necessary. You'll also need an assortment of Sharps for handwork and quilting needles (#8, #9, or #10) if you plan to hand quilt.

Pins: Multicolored glass or plastic-headed pins are generally longer, stronger, and easier to see and hold than regular dressmaker's pins.

Iron and Ironing Board: A shot of steam is useful.

Seam Ripper: I always keep one handy.

How to Make a Quilt

Information on choosing and preparing fabrics, cutting, and piecing Feathered Star blocks begins on page 54. The information given here includes how to finish the whole quilt and a few techniques that are useful for piecing Feathered Star quilts.

Strip-Piecing

A few Feathered Star quilts pictured in the first part of this book, have triple-striped lattices with nine-patch corner-stones. It is easiest to piece these sections with strip-piecing.

Strip-piecing is a method for quickly sewing patchwork units together by machine. Long fabric strips are sewn together in units called strata and then cut into shorter portions; the small units are then recombined to form simple designs. The technique is similar to Seminole piecing, but here the shapes are usually used in traditional patchwork instead of decorative bands for clothing and other projects.

Straight-Grain Strip-Piecing

Use straight-grain strip-piecing when working with squares and rectangles. For instance, to make the triple lattice sections in the Feathered Star Sampler on page 12, three long strips (red, white, red) were sewn together, then cut to the proper length.

It is best to cut strips from the lengthwise grain of the fabric. When it is necessary to use the cross-grain to get the required length, be sure to straighten the fabric so strips will be cut exactly on-grain.

Press the fabric well before cutting strips. The accuracy of the piecing will depend largely on how carefully fabric, strips, and seams are pressed.

To determine the width to cut strips, add a 1/4" seam allowance to each side of the finished strip. For example, if the finished dimension of the piece will be 1", cut 1 1/2" strips. Stack the fabric before marking and cutting so two or four layers can be cut at one time. Mark strips and cut with sharp scissors or a rotary cutter. Try to be accurate; speed-piecing does not mean sloppy piecing.

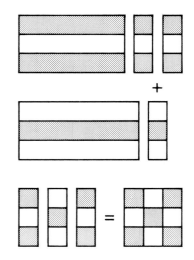

Sew long strips together with 1/4" seam allowances, but wait to press until all the strips in the unit have been sewn. Press seam allowances toward the darker fabric, and press from the right side of the work so the fabric won't pleat along the seam lines. Use templates or simply measure distances to mark locations for crosswise cuts.

Setting the Quilt Together

After the Feathered Star blocks are pieced, you are ready to "set" them together to make the quilt top. Sets for Feathered Star quilts are discussed beginning on page 21.

Sew the completed blocks and set pieces (lattice strips and cornerstones or alternate squares) together in rows. Then join the rows together. When the center portion of the quilt top is set together, borders may be added.

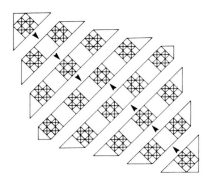

Assembly sequence of diagonally set quilt

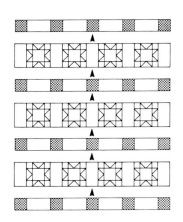

Assembly sequence with lattices and cornerstones

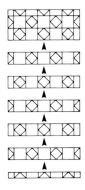

Assembly sequence of a bar quilt

Borders

If you choose plain borders with straight-sewn corners, first sew borders to the long sides of the quilt, then to the width. Striped fabrics make lovely quilt borders, but the corner must be mitered to make the design turn the corner gracefully. Mitering corners is not difficult and worth the effort in many design situations. It is especially important to miter corners when using strips of multiple plain borders.

Mitering Corners

1. Prepare the borders. Determine the finished outside dimensions of your quilt. Cut the borders this length plus 1/2" for seam allowances. When using a striped fabric for the borders, make sure the design on all four borders is cut the same way. Multiple borders should be sewn together and the resulting "striped" units treated as a single border for mitering.

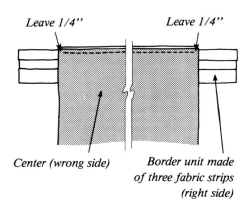

Leave 1/4"   *Leave 1/4"*

Center (wrong side)   *Border unit made of three fabric strips (right side)*

2. To attach the border to the pieced section of the quilt, center each border on a side so the ends extend equally on either side of the center section. Using a 1/4" seam allowance, sew the border to the center, leaving 1/4" unsewn at the beginning and end of the stitching line. Press the seam allowances toward the border.

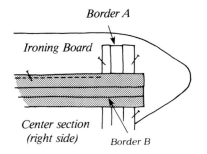

Border A

Ironing Board

Center section (right side)   *Border B*

3. Arrange the first corner to be mitered on the ironing board as illustrated. Press the corner flat and straight. To prevent it from slipping, pin the quilt to the ironing board. Following the illustration, turn border "B" right side up, folding the corner to be mitered under at a 45° angle. Match the raw edges underneath with those of border "A". Fuss with it until it looks good. The stripes and border designs should meet. Check the squareness of the corner with a right angle. Press the fold. This will be the sewing line. Pin the borders together to prevent shifting and unpin the piece from the board. Turn wrong side out and pin along the fold line, readjusting if necessary to match the designs.

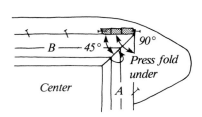

B — 45°   90°

Press fold under

Center   *A*

4. Machine baste from the inside to the outside corner on the fold line, leaving 1/4" at the beginning unsewn. Check for accuracy. If it is right, sew again with a regular stitch. Backtack at the beginning and end of the stitching line. (After you have mitered several times, the basting step ceases to be necessary.) Trim the excess fabric 1/4" along the mitered seam. Press this seam open. Press the other seams to the outside.

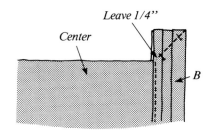

Leave 1/4"

Center   *B*

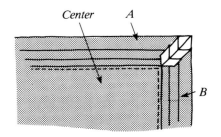

Center   *A*

B

Preparing to Quilt

Marking

In most cases, before you quilt, the quilt top must be marked with lines to guide stitching. Where you place the quilting lines will depend on the patchwork design, the type of batting used, and how much quilting you want to do. You can mark an allover, straight-line pattern, such as a grid of squares or parallel diagonal lines. Or, you can outline quilt the design either "in the ditch" (close to but not on the seam lines) or 1/4" away on each side of every seam line, for which no marking is required. There are many pretty, traditional quilting motifs that fit nicely in plain areas, such as unpieced blocks and borders. Try to avoid quilting too close to the seam lines, where the bulk of seam allowances might slow you down or make the stitches uneven. Also keep in mind that the purpose of quilting, besides its aesthetic value, is to securely hold the three layers together. Don't leave large areas unquilted.

Thoroughly press the quilt top and mark it, before it is assembled with the batting and backing. You will need marking pencils, a long ruler or yardstick, stencils or templates for quilting motifs, and a smooth, clean, hard surface on which to work. Use a sharp marking pencil and lightly mark the quilting lines on the fabric. No matter what kind of marking tool is used, light lines will be easier to remove than heavy ones.

Backing

A single length of 45"-wide fabric can often be used for backing small quilts. To be safe, plan on a usable width of only 42" after shrinkage and cutting off selvages. For larger quilts, two lengths of fabric will have to be sewn together to get one large enough.

Cut the backing 1" larger than the quilt top all the way around. Press thoroughly with seams open. Lay the backing face down on a large, clean, flat surface. With masking tape, tape the backing down (without stretching) to keep it smooth and flat while you are working with the other layers.

Batting

Batting is the filler in a quilt or comforter. Thick batting is used in comforters that are tied. If you plan to quilt, use thin batting and quilt by hand.

Thin batting comes in 100% polyester, 100% cotton, and a cotton-polyester (80%-20%) combination. All cotton batting requires close quilting to prevent shifting and separating in the wash. Most old quilts have cotton batting and are rather flat. Cotton is a good natural fiber that lasts well and is compatible with cotton and cotton-blend fabrics. Less quilting is required on 100% polyester batting. If polyester batting is glazed or bonded, it is easy to work with, won't pull apart, and has more loft than cotton. Some polyester batting, however, has a tendency to "beard." This "fiber migration" (the small white polyester fibers creep to the quilt's surface between the threads in the fabric) happens mostly when polyester blends are used instead of 100% cotton fabrics. The cotton-polyester combination batting is supposed to combine the best features of the two fibers. A single layer of preshrunk cotton flannel can be used for filler instead of batting. The quilt will be very flat, and the quilting stitches highly visible.

Cut the batting the same size as the quilt backing and lay it gently on top.

Assembling the Layers

Center the freshly ironed and marked quilt top on top of the batting, face up. Starting in the middle, pin baste the three layers together while gently smoothing out fullness to the sides and corners. Take care not to distort the straight lines of the quilt design and the borders.

After pinning, baste the layers together with needle and light-colored thread. Start in the middle and make a line of large stitches to each corner to form a large X. Continue basting in a grid of parallel lines 6" to 8" apart. Finish with a row of basting around the outside edges. Quilts to be quilted with a hoop or on your lap will be handled more than those quilted on a frame; therefore, they will require more basting.

After basting, remove the pins. Now you are ready to quilt.

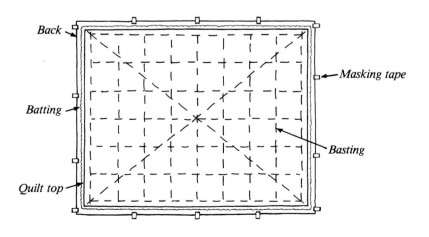

Back — *Batting* — *Quilt top* — *Masking tape* — *Basting*

Hand Quilting

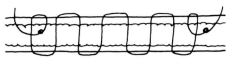

Hand-quilting stitch

To quilt by hand, you will need quilting thread, quilting needles, small scissors, a thimble, and perhaps a balloon or large rubber band to help grasp the needle if it gets stuck. Quilt on a frame, a large hoop, or just on your lap or a table. Use a single strand of quilting thread not longer than 18''. Make a small single knot in the end of the thread. The quilting stitch is a small running stitch that goes through all three layers of the quilt. Take two, three, or even four stitches at a time if you can keep them even. When crossing seams, you might find it necessary to "hunt and peck" one stitch at a time.

To begin, insert the needle in the top layer about 3/4'' from the point you want to start stitching. Pull the needle out at the starting point and gently tug at the knot until it pops through the fabric and is buried in the batting. Make a backstitch and begin quilting. Stitches should be tiny (8 to 10 per inch is good), even, and straight. At first, concentrate on even and straight; tiny will come with practice.

When you come almost to the end of the thread, make a single knot fairly close to the fabric. Make a backstitch to bury the knot in the batting. Run the thread off through the batting and out the quilt top. Snip it off. The first and last stitches look different from the running stitches between. To make them less noticeable, start and stop where quilting lines cross each other or at seam joints.

Binding

After quilting, trim excess batting and backing to the edge of the quilt front. Finish the raw edges with bias binding. Bias binding can be purchased by the package or by the yard, or you can make your own.

To make bias binding from yardage, press a single layer of fabric. Use a 12'' right angle to establish the bias (45° angle) of the fabric by aligning one of the angle's short sides with the selvage. Draw a line on the fabric along the 45° angle. Using this first marked line as a guide, draw several more parallel lines, each 2'' apart. You'll find the 2''-wide plastic ruler very handy for this procedure. Cut the strips and seam them together where necessary to get a bias strip long enough for each side of the quilt (the length of the side plus 2'').

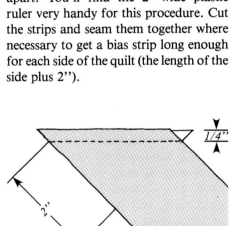

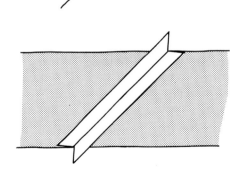

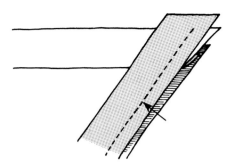

Overlapping bias binding at quilt corners

Using the "even-feed" presser foot and a 1/2'' seam allowance, sew the binding strips to the front of the quilt. Be careful not to stretch the bias or the quilt edge as you sew. If your machine doesn't have an "even-feed" foot, sometimes it is best to put the binding on entirely by hand. Overlap the corners. Fold under the raw edge of the binding on the back side of the quilt. Pin it in place. Enclose the raw edges at the corners. Using thread to match the binding, hand sew the binding in place with a hemming stitch.

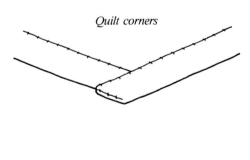

Quilt corners

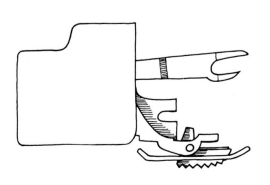

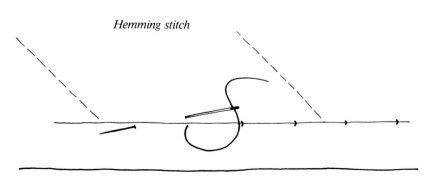

Hemming stitch

BIBLIOGRAPHY

Albacete, M.J.; D'Atri, Sharon; and Reeves, Jan. OHIO QUILTS: A LIVING TRADITION. Canton, OH: The Canton Art Institute, 1981.

The Art Institute of Chicago. AMERICAN QUILTS. Chicago: Chicago Art Institute, 1966.

Bacon, Lenice Ingram. AMERICAN PATCHWORK QUILTS. New York: William Morrow & Company, Inc., 1973.

Benberry, Cuesta. "The 20th Century's First Quilt Revival." QUILTERS NEWSLETTER MAGAZINE, October 1979, p. 10.

Beyer, Alice. QUILTING. Chicago: South Park Commissioners, 1934.

Beyer, Jinny. PATCHWORK PATTERNS. McLean, VA: EPM Publications, Inc., 1979.

Beyer, Jinny. THE QUILTER'S ALBUM OF BLOCK AND BORDERS. McLean, VA: EPM Publications, Inc., 1980.

Binney, Edwin, 3d and Binney-Winslow, Gail. HOMAGE TO AMANDA. San Francisco: R. K. Press, 1984.

Bishop, Robert. NEW DISCOVERIES IN AMERICAN QUILTS. New York: E. P. Dutton, Inc., 1975.

Bishop, Robert; Secord, William; and Weissman, Judith Reiter. QUILTS, COVERLETS, RUGS AND SAMPLERS. New York: Alfred A. Knopf, 1982.

Brackman, Barbara. AN ENCYCLOPEDIA OF PERIOD QUILT PATTERNS, Volume V. Lawrence, KS, 1981.

Bresenhan, Karoline Patterson and Puentes, Nancy O'Bryant. LONE STARS: A LEGACY OF TEXAS QUILTS, 1836-1936. Austin, TX: University of Texas Press, 1986.

----, "California Star Quilt." McCALL'S SUPER BOOK OF QUILTING, 1976, p. 52.

Carlisle, Lillian Baker. QUILTS AT THE SHELBURNE MUSEUM. Shelburne, VT: The Shelburne Museum, 1957.

Earle, Alice Morse. HOME LIFE IN COLONIAL DAYS. New York: The Macmillan Co., 1910.

Ericson, Helen M. "Quilt Topics — Feathered and Sawtooth Stars." TELEGRAPHICS, 28 September 1983, p. 2A.

----, "Feather Edge Star." KANSAS CITY STAR, 11 August 1934.

----, "Feathered Christmas Star." LADY'S CIRCLE PATCHWORK QUILTS, no. 17, (1979), p. 25.

----, "Feathered Stars." LADY'S CIRCLE PATCHWORK QUILTS, Winter 1982, p. 32.

Finley, Ruth E. OLD PATCHWORK QUILTS AND THE WOMEN WHO MADE THEM. Newton Center, MA: Charles T. Branford Company, 1929.

Gross, Joyce, "Cuesta Benberry: Part II, Significant Milestones for Quilters." QUILTERS JOURNAL, no. 24, (1984), p. 8.

Hagerman, Betty J. and Ericson, Helen M., ed. KANSAS QUILT SYMPOSIUM, Lawrence, KS: Kaw Valley Quilter's Guild, 1978.

Hall, Carrie A. and Kretsinger, Rose G. THE ROMANCE OF THE PATCHWORK QUILT. New York: Bonanza Books, 1935.

Holstein, Jonathan. THE PIECED QUILT, AN AMERICAN DESIGN TRADITION. Greenwich, CT: New York Graphic Society, Ltd., 1973.

Irwin, John Rice, A PEOPLE AND THEIR QUILTS. Exton, PA: Schiffer Publishing Company, 1983.

----, KANSAS QUILT TREASURES II. Logan, KS: The Dane G. Hanson Memorial Museum, 1983.

Kile, Michael M., ed. THE QUILT DIGEST-3. San Francisco: The Quilt Digest Press, 1985.

Lane, Rose Wilder. WOMAN'S DAY BOOK OF AMERICAN NEEDLEWORK. New York: Simon & Schuster, 1963.

Mainardi, Patricia. QUILTS, THE GREAT AMERICAN ART. San Pedro, CA: Miles and Weir, Ltd., 1978.

Martin, Judy. "Fine Feathered Star." QUILTMAKER, Fall/Winter 1986, p. 24.

Martin, Judy. PATCHWORKBOOK. New York: Charles Scribner's Sons, 1983.

Martin, Nancy J. PIECES OF THE PAST. Bothell, WA: That Patchwork Place, Inc., 1986.

McCloskey, Marsha R. CHRISTMAS QUILTS. Bothell, WA: That Patchwork Place, Inc., 1985.

McCloskey, Marsha R. "The Feathered Star." THE FLYING NEEDLE, May 1985, p. 20.

McCloskey, Marsha R. FEATHERED STAR SAMPLER. Bothell, WA: That Patchwork Place, Inc., 1985.

McCloskey, Marsha R., "Great American Quilt Classics: Feathered Star Quilts." QUILTER'S NEWSLETTER MAGAZINE. September 1986, p. 19.

McCloskey, Marsha R. "Star Spangled Banner." LADY'S CIRCLE PATCHWORK QUILTS. May 1985, p. 47.

McKim, Ruby. 101 PATCHWORK PATTERNS. New York: Dover Publications, Inc., 1962.

Meeker, L. K. QUILT PATTERNS FOR THE COLLECTOR. Portland, OR: L. K. Meeker, 1979.

Meldrum, Alex, ed. IRISH PATCHWORK. Dublin, Ireland: Allied Irish Banks, 1979.

Nelson, Cyril I. THE QUILT ENGAGEMENT CALENDAR. New York: E. P. Dutton, Inc., 1980, 1981, 1983.

Nelson, Cyril I. and Houck, Carter. THE QUILT ENGAGEMENT CALENDAR TREASURY. New York: E.P. Dutton, Inc., 1982.

----, "Old Time Quilting — Feathered Star." QUILTER'S NEWSLETTER MAGAZINE, May 1977, p. 18.

Orlofsky, Patsy and Myron. QUILTS IN AMERICA. New York: McGraw-Hill Book Co., 1974.

Penny, Prudence. OLD TIME QUILTS. Seattle, WA: Seattle Post-Intelligencer, 1927.

Peto, Florence. HISTORIC QUILTS. New York: The American Historical Company, Inc., 1939.

----, "Pine Cone." KANSAS CITY STAR, 23 October 1935.

----, QUILTS, A TRADITION OF VARIATIONS. Exhibition Catalog, Albany, CA: East Bay Heritage Quilters, 1982.

----, "Radiant Star." FAVORITES — OLD AND NEW, A NEW BOOK OF 35 QUILT PATTERNS, Aunt Martha's Catalog, 1932.

Ramsey, Bets and Waldvogel, Merikay. THE QUILTS OF TENNESSEE. Nashville, Tennessee: Rutledge Hill Press, 1986.

Safford, Carleton L. and Bishop, Robert. AMERICA'S QUILTS AND COVERLETS. New York: Weathervane Books, 1974.

128

Strasser, Susan. NEVER DONE: A HISTORY OF AMERICAN HOUSEWORK. New York: Pantheon Books, 1982.
Stratton, Joanna L. PIONEER WOMEN: VOICES FROM THE KANSAS FRONTIER. New York: Simon & Schuster, 1981.
Troianello, Ann, Project Chairman. A COMMON THREAD: QUILTS IN THE YAKIMA VALLEY. Yakima, WA: Yakima Valley Museum and Historical Association, 1985.
----, "A Very Old Sawtooth Quilt." KANSAS CITY STAR, 1929.
Webster, Marie D. QUILTS: THEIR STORY AND HOW TO MAKE THEM. Garden City, NY: Doubleday Page & Company, 1916.
----, "What's New." QUILTER'S NEWSLETTER MAGAZINE: March 1987, p. 6.

ORDERING INFORMATION

"Fine Feathered Star" pattern appears in *Quiltmaker* magazine, Fall/Winter 1986. For information, write to Quiltmaker, 6700 West 44th Ave., Wheatridge, Colorado 80034.

"Pattern 32, Feathered Star" is in the *Stearns and Foster Catalog of Quilt Pattern Designs and Needlecraft Supplies*. For information, write to The Stearns Technical Textiles Company, Consumer Products Division, 100 Williams St., Cincinnati, Ohio 45215.

PHOTO CREDITS

George Champlin, OHS Chief Photographer, pp. 35, 41, 43; Jerry Felice, pp. 12, 26, 36; Roy Hale, p. 24; Skip Howard, cover, pp. 1, 2, 5, 9, 13, 16, 18, 22, 27, 28, 32, 37, 39, 40, 42-46, 54, 57; David Luttrel, p. 38; Phil McCrady, p. 46; Jack Mathieson, pp. 27, 40; Carl Murray, pp. 9, 12, 14, 15, 19, 20, 26, 34, 37; Sharon Risedorph with Lynn Kellner, p. 49; Larry Schwarm, p. 30; Steve Tuttle, pp. 33, 41.

Illustration and Graphics . . . . Stephanie Benson
Marsha McCloskey

Marsha McCloskey is an internationally known quiltmaker, teacher and author of numerous quilt books. She is known for her precise machine piecing, rotary-cutting techniques and love of traditional quilt designs. Marsha lives in Seattle, Washington and travels to teach and lecture wherever quiltmaking takes her.

Other Books by Marsha McCloskey
Feathered Star Sampler
100 Pieced Patterns for 8" Quilt Blocks
Guide to Rotary Cutting
On to Square Two
Lessons in Machine Piecing
Stars and Stepping Stones
Christmas Quilts
Projects for Blocks and Borders
Wall Quilts
Small Quilts
by Marsha McCloskey and Judy Martin
Pieced Borders: The Complete Resource
by Marsha McCloskey, Mary Hickey, Sara Nephew and Nancy J. Martin
Quick and Easy Quiltmaking
by Marsha McCloskey and Nancy J. Martin
Ocean Waves
A Dozen Variables

For prices, availability and ordering information for Marsha McCloskey's books, contact:

FEATHERED STAR PRODUCTIONS
2151 7th Avenue West
Seattle, Washington 98119
Phone/Fax (206)283-5214